IaaS Mastery

Infrastructure As A Aervice

Your All-In-One Guide To AWS, GCE, Microsoft Azure, and IBM Cloud

4 BOOKS IN 1

Book 1
IaaS Fundamentals: A Beginner's Guide to Cloud Infrastructure

Book 2
Mastering IaaS: Building Scalable Cloud Solutions with AWS and GCE

Book 3
Advanced IaaS Architectures: Optimizing Microsoft Azure for Enterprises

Book 4
IaaS Expertise: Harnessing the Power of IBM Cloud for Enterprise Solutions

ROB BOTWRIGHT

Published by Rob Botwright
Library of Congress Cataloging-in-Publication Data
ISBN 978-1-83938-585-8
Cover design by Rizzo

Disclaimer

The contents of this book are based on extensive research and the best available historical sources. However, the author and publisher make no claims, promises, or guarantees about the accuracy, completeness, or adequacy of the information contained herein. The information in this book is provided on an "as is" basis, and the author and publisher disclaim any and all liability for any errors, omissions, or inaccuracies in the information or for any actions taken in reliance on such information.

The opinions and views expressed in this book are those of the author and do not necessarily reflect the official policy or position of any organization or individual mentioned in this book. Any reference to specific people, places, or events is intended only to provide historical context and is not intended to defame or malign any group, individual, or entity.

The information in this book is intended for educational and entertainment purposes only. It is not intended to be a substitute for professional advice or judgment. Readers are encouraged to conduct their own research and to seek professional advice where appropriate.

Every effort has been made to obtain necessary permissions and acknowledgments for all images and other copyrighted material used in this book. Any errors or omissions in this regard are unintentional, and the author and publisher will correct them in future editions.

Book 1 - IaaS Fundamentals: A Beginner's Guide to Cloud Infrastructure

Book 2 - Mastering IaaS: Building Scalable Cloud Solutions with AWS and GCE

Book 3 - Advanced IaaS Architectures: Optimizing Microsoft Azure for Enterprises

Book 4 - IaaS Expertise: Harnessing the Power of IBM Cloud for Enterprise Solutions

Introduction

In the rapidly evolving landscape of technology, the cloud has emerged as a transformative force, reshaping the way businesses operate, innovate, and scale. Within the vast realm of cloud computing, Infrastructure as a Service (IaaS) stands as the foundation upon which modern digital infrastructures are built. It is the cornerstone of flexibility, scalability, and efficiency in the digital age.

Welcome to "IaaS Mastery: Infrastructure as a Service," an all-encompassing book bundle that serves as your compass in navigating the intricate world of cloud infrastructure. In this carefully curated collection, we bring you four volumes designed to take you from the very basics to the pinnacle of expertise in IaaS. Together, we will embark on a journey that covers the essential concepts, practical implementations, advanced architectures, and the specialized prowess needed to harness the capabilities of the world's leading cloud providers.

Book 1 - IaaS Fundamentals: A Beginner's Guide to Cloud Infrastructure:
Our journey begins with the foundational volume, where we cater to both newcomers and those seeking a comprehensive review of cloud essentials. In this book, we lay the groundwork for your exploration of IaaS by demystifying complex cloud concepts, elucidating the key benefits of cloud computing, and guiding you through the core principles that underpin IaaS. It is here that you'll build a solid foundation upon which the subsequent volumes will be constructed.

Book 2 - Mastering IaaS: Building Scalable Cloud Solutions with AWS and GCE:
With the fundamentals firmly established, we transition into the practical realm of IaaS by exploring two of the most prominent cloud service providers: Amazon Web Services (AWS) and Google Cloud Engine (GCE). This volume equips you with the knowledge and hands-on experience required to create scalable and resilient cloud solutions using AWS and GCE. Dive into the intricacies of resource provisioning, management, and optimization in these environments.

Book 3 - Advanced IaaS Architectures: Optimizing Microsoft Azure for Enterprises:
Advancing further into the IaaS ecosystem, the third book takes an enterprise-centric approach by focusing on Microsoft Azure. Here, we delve into the complexities of high-performance networks, scalable compute solutions, advanced security measures, and automation strategies tailored specifically for enterprise-grade workloads. This volume prepares you to tackle the intricate challenges faced by organizations operating at scale within the Azure cloud.

Book 4 - IaaS Expertise: Harnessing the Power of IBM Cloud for Enterprise Solutions:
Our journey culminates in the fourth volume, where we explore the unique capabilities of IBM Cloud as a potent tool for enterprise transformation. In this book, you will uncover the wealth of infrastructure offerings, networking strategies, security features, and advanced automation capabilities provided by IBM Cloud. Real-world enterprise success stories will provide you with valuable insights into the tangible impact of IBM Cloud on large organizations.

In this book bundle, we aim to empower you with the knowledge and skills required to thrive in an era where cloud infrastructure is the linchpin of digital transformation. Whether you are an aspiring cloud enthusiast, a seasoned IT professional seeking to refine your skills, or an enterprise leader looking to leverage cloud technology for competitive advantage, this bundle is your all-in-one guide to mastering IaaS.

Prepare to embark on a journey that will broaden your horizons, enhance your technical prowess, and equip you with the expertise needed to navigate the ever-evolving world of cloud infrastructure. "IaaS Mastery: Infrastructure as a Service" is your gateway to unlocking the boundless potential of cloud computing, and we are thrilled to embark on this transformative journey with you.

Book 1
IaaS Fundamentals
A Beginner's Guide to Cloud Infrastructure

ROB BOTWRIGHT

Chapter 1: Understanding Cloud Computing Basics

In today's ever-evolving technological landscape, cloud computing has emerged as a transformative force that has revolutionized the way individuals, businesses, and organizations approach information technology and data management. The concept of cloud computing has fundamentally altered the traditional paradigms of on-premises computing, offering a dynamic and flexible alternative that allows users to access and leverage a vast array of computing resources over the internet. This shift towards cloud computing has been driven by a compelling set of advantages, ranging from cost efficiency and scalability to enhanced accessibility and collaboration. As we embark on this journey into the world of cloud computing, it is essential to gain a comprehensive understanding of its fundamental principles, underlying technologies, and the diverse range of services and deployment models it encompasses.

At its core, cloud computing represents a fundamental shift from owning and managing physical hardware and software to utilizing virtualized resources provided by cloud service providers. These resources include computing power, storage, networking, and a multitude of software services that are delivered over the internet on a pay-as-you-go basis. This transformation has heralded a new era of flexibility, agility, and cost-effectiveness in the realm of IT infrastructure. Whether you are a small startup, a multinational corporation, or an individual user, cloud computing offers a compelling value proposition that can be tailored to your specific needs and requirements.

One of the central pillars of cloud computing is the concept of resource pooling, where computing resources are shared and allocated dynamically to multiple users on a multi-tenant model. This approach ensures efficient utilization of resources, reducing wastage and optimizing costs. In addition to resource pooling, cloud computing also embodies the principles of self-service and rapid elasticity. Users have the ability to provision and deprovision resources as needed, scaling up or down in response to changing workloads and demands. This elasticity is a key driver of cost savings and operational efficiency in the cloud.

Cloud computing services can be categorized into three primary service models: Infrastructure as a Service (IaaS), Platform as a Service (PaaS), and Software as a Service (SaaS). Each of these models offers a distinct set of services and capabilities tailored to different user needs. IaaS provides users with the fundamental building blocks of computing, such as virtual machines, storage, and networking resources. PaaS goes a step further by offering a platform and development environment that enables users to build, deploy, and manage applications without the complexities of infrastructure management. Finally, SaaS delivers fully-fledged software applications that can be accessed over the internet, eliminating the need for local installations and maintenance.

In addition to service models, cloud computing offers various deployment models that dictate how cloud resources are hosted and accessed. The most common deployment models are the public cloud, private cloud, hybrid cloud, and multi-cloud. Public clouds are owned and operated by cloud service providers and are available to the general public, providing a cost-effective and scalable solution for a wide range of applications. Private clouds, on the other hand, are dedicated to a single organization and can be hosted on-premises or by a third-party provider. Private clouds offer greater control and security, making them suitable for businesses with stringent compliance and data protection requirements. Hybrid clouds combine elements of both public and private clouds, allowing data and applications to move seamlessly between them.

Multi-cloud strategies involve the use of multiple cloud providers to avoid vendor lock-in and optimize cost and performance.

Security and compliance are paramount concerns in cloud computing, as organizations entrust cloud service providers with their sensitive data and critical workloads. Cloud providers invest heavily in security measures, including data encryption, access controls, and threat detection, to safeguard their infrastructure and customer data. However, the responsibility for securing data and applications in the cloud is a shared responsibility between the provider and the user. Organizations must implement their security measures, policies, and governance frameworks to ensure a robust security posture in the cloud.

Moreover, compliance with industry regulations and standards is a critical consideration, especially for businesses operating in highly regulated sectors such as healthcare, finance, and government. Cloud providers often offer compliance certifications and attestations to demonstrate their adherence to specific security and compliance standards. However, organizations must conduct due diligence and assess whether the chosen cloud provider aligns with their compliance requirements.

The cloud computing landscape is continually evolving, driven by rapid advancements in technology and an ever-expanding array of services and capabilities. Emerging technologies such as serverless computing, containerization, and edge computing are reshaping the cloud landscape, offering new possibilities for application development and deployment. Serverless computing allows developers to build and run applications without managing servers, reducing operational overhead and enabling more efficient use of resources. Containerization, on the other hand, provides a lightweight and portable way to package and deploy applications, fostering consistency across different cloud environments. Edge computing brings computation closer to the data source, reducing latency and enabling real-time processing for applications in areas such as IoT and autonomous vehicles.

As we explore the intricacies of cloud computing, it becomes evident that the cloud is not a one-size-fits-all solution. Rather, it is a dynamic ecosystem that can be tailored to address specific business challenges and opportunities. Whether you are a startup looking to rapidly scale your web application, an enterprise seeking to modernize legacy systems, or a researcher harnessing the power of artificial intelligence, cloud computing provides a versatile and powerful toolkit to meet your objectives.

In the chapters that follow, we will delve deeper into the various facets of cloud computing, from the fundamental building blocks of cloud infrastructure to the practical considerations of migrating to and managing resources in the cloud. We will explore the strategies and best practices for optimizing cost and performance, as well as the tools and services that facilitate cloud-native application development and deployment. Moreover, we will examine real-world case studies and success stories that showcase the transformative potential of cloud computing in diverse industries and scenarios.

The journey into the world of cloud computing is an exciting one, filled with opportunities for innovation, efficiency, and growth. Whether you are embarking on your cloud journey as a newcomer or looking to expand your cloud expertise, this book will serve as a valuable guide, equipping you with the knowledge and insights needed to navigate the cloud landscape effectively. Together, we will unravel the complexities of cloud computing, demystify its key concepts, and empower you to harness its full potential for your personal or organizational success.

The historical evolution of cloud computing is a fascinating journey through the annals of computing and information technology. It represents a significant paradigm shift that has reshaped the way we store, access, and process data. To truly appreciate the present state of cloud computing, it is essential to delve into its historical roots and trace the milestones that have led to its emergence as a ubiquitous and transformative technology.

The concept of cloud computing can be traced back to the mid-20th century when early computer scientists and engineers began envisioning a future where computing resources could be accessed remotely and shared among multiple users. During this era, large mainframe computers dominated the computing landscape, and users interacted with these centralized systems through terminals connected over networks.

In the 1960s, the idea of utility computing emerged as a precursor to cloud computing. John McCarthy, an American computer scientist, famously remarked that "computation may someday be organized as a public utility," envisioning a time when computing power would be as accessible and affordable as electricity. However, it would take several decades for this vision to become a reality.

The birth of the internet in the late 20th century was a pivotal moment in the evolution of cloud computing. The internet provided the infrastructure and connectivity needed to realize the vision of remote computing resources. In the 1990s, internet-based services like Application Service Providers (ASPs) began offering software applications over the internet, marking an early step towards cloud-based software delivery.

The term "cloud computing" itself started gaining traction in the early 2000s, although the concept had been evolving for decades. Amazon Web Services (AWS), launched in 2006, played a pivotal role in popularizing cloud computing as a scalable and cost-effective solution for businesses. AWS offered a range of cloud services, including computing power and storage, on a pay-as-you-go model.

The emergence of virtualization technology was another key milestone in the history of cloud computing. Virtualization allowed multiple virtual machines (VMs) to run on a single physical server, enabling better resource utilization and flexibility. This technology laid the foundation for the creation of cloud infrastructure as we know it today.

In addition to AWS, other tech giants like Google and Microsoft recognized the potential of cloud computing and entered the market with their respective cloud platforms, Google Cloud Platform (GCP) and Microsoft Azure. These companies leveraged their expertise in data centers, networking, and software to build robust and comprehensive cloud ecosystems.

The rise of cloud computing coincided with the explosion of data and the need for scalable storage solutions. Cloud storage services like Amazon S3 and Google Cloud Storage provided businesses with affordable and reliable options for storing vast amounts of data in the cloud. This shift towards cloud-based storage marked a departure from traditional on-premises data centers.

As cloud computing gained momentum, it began to reshape the way businesses operated. Startups and enterprises alike leveraged the cloud to launch new services, scale their infrastructure, and reduce the costs and complexities associated with managing on-premises hardware. Cloud computing offered agility, allowing businesses to respond quickly to changing market dynamics and customer demands.

The introduction of cloud-based Software as a Service (SaaS) applications revolutionized how individuals and organizations accessed and used software. Services like Salesforce, Dropbox, and Microsoft Office 365 provided users with the flexibility to use software applications over the internet without the need for installation or maintenance.

The cloud also facilitated the emergence of new technologies and paradigms, such as Big Data and analytics. Data scientists and businesses leveraged cloud-based platforms to process and analyze massive datasets, gaining insights that were previously inaccessible. Cloud-based machine learning services further accelerated the adoption of artificial intelligence and predictive analytics.

Security and compliance in the cloud became paramount concerns as businesses entrusted cloud providers with their sensitive data and workloads. Cloud providers invested heavily in security measures, including encryption, access controls, and threat detection, to protect their infrastructure and customer data. Compliance certifications and attestations became important benchmarks for cloud providers to demonstrate their commitment to security and regulatory requirements.

The concept of serverless computing emerged as a breakthrough in cloud architecture. Serverless platforms allowed developers to focus on writing code without the need to manage servers or infrastructure. Functions as a Service (FaaS) offerings like AWS Lambda and Azure Functions exemplified the serverless approach, enabling event-driven and highly scalable applications.

Edge computing, an extension of cloud computing, brought computation closer to the data source. This paradigm shift reduced latency and enabled real-time processing for applications in areas such as the Internet of Things (IoT) and autonomous vehicles. Edge computing allowed devices to process data locally, reducing the need for data to travel long distances to centralized data centers.

In recent years, containerization technologies like Docker and Kubernetes gained popularity in the cloud ecosystem. Containers provided a lightweight and portable way to package and deploy applications, making it easier to manage and scale applications across diverse cloud environments.

Looking ahead, the evolution of cloud computing continues. Emerging technologies such as quantum computing hold the promise of solving complex problems at speeds previously unimaginable. Multi-cloud strategies are becoming more prevalent, allowing organizations to leverage multiple cloud providers to avoid vendor lock-in and optimize cost and performance.

The historical evolution of cloud computing showcases the relentless march of technology and innovation. From the early dreams of utility computing to the present-day realities of cloud-native architectures and serverless computing, cloud technology has evolved to meet the changing needs of businesses and individuals. As we navigate this dynamic landscape, it is essential to understand the historical context that has shaped the cloud computing industry and its profound impact on the world of technology and business.

In the chapters that follow, we will delve deeper into the core concepts, service models, deployment models, and practical considerations of cloud computing. We will explore the strategies and best practices for harnessing the power of the cloud, whether you are an entrepreneur launching a startup, an IT professional managing enterprise infrastructure, or a data scientist exploring the frontiers of artificial intelligence. Our journey through the cloud computing landscape will equip you with the knowledge and insights needed to leverage cloud technology effectively and drive innovation in your endeavors.

Chapter 2: Introduction to Infrastructure as a Service (IaaS)

Infrastructure as a Service, commonly referred to as IaaS, is a fundamental component of cloud computing that has revolutionized the way organizations procure and manage their IT infrastructure. It represents a model where computing resources such as virtual machines, storage, and networking are provided over the internet on a pay-as-you-go basis, offering unparalleled flexibility and scalability. At its core, IaaS aims to abstract and virtualize the underlying hardware, enabling users to access and control their infrastructure resources remotely. This abstraction liberates organizations from the constraints of physical hardware and empowers them to build, deploy, and manage their applications and services with ease.

The essence of IaaS lies in its ability to deliver infrastructure resources as a service, eliminating the need for organizations to invest in and maintain on-premises hardware. Instead, users can leverage the cloud to provision and manage virtualized resources according to their specific requirements. This shift from capital-intensive, on-premises infrastructure to an operational expenditure model has significant financial implications, allowing organizations to optimize costs and allocate resources more efficiently.

A defining characteristic of IaaS is the concept of resource pooling, where computing resources are shared and allocated dynamically to multiple users in a multi-tenant environment. This efficient utilization of resources minimizes waste and results in cost savings for both providers and users. Resource pooling also ensures that users can scale their infrastructure up or down rapidly in response to changing workloads, without the need for long procurement cycles or upfront investments.

One of the key benefits of IaaS is the elimination of the burden associated with hardware procurement and maintenance. Traditional data centers require organizations to purchase, install, and manage physical servers, storage arrays, and networking equipment. In contrast, IaaS providers manage the physical infrastructure, including server farms, data centers, and networking gear, relieving users of the responsibility of hardware upkeep and replacement.

The self-service aspect of IaaS empowers users to provision and manage their infrastructure resources independently. This self-service model allows for agility and flexibility in resource allocation, as users can rapidly adapt to changing business needs without relying on IT departments or external vendors. It promotes a culture of empowerment and innovation within organizations, as development and operations teams can quickly experiment, deploy, and scale applications to meet business objectives.

IaaS providers offer a wide range of services and components that enable users to build and customize their infrastructure environments. Virtual machines (VMs) serve as the fundamental building blocks, providing compute capacity with various operating systems and configurations. Users can select from a catalog of VM sizes and types to match their specific application requirements.

Storage is another critical component of IaaS, offering various options such as block storage for data volumes, object storage for scalable and durable file storage, and file storage for shared file systems. Networking services provide the necessary connectivity and security for applications, including virtual networks, load balancers, firewalls, and VPNs.

Scalability is a core tenet of IaaS, allowing users to adjust the size and capacity of their infrastructure resources as demand fluctuates. This capability ensures that organizations can handle traffic spikes, accommodate growth, and optimize resource utilization. Auto-scaling features further automate the process by automatically adjusting resource allocation based on predefined policies and triggers.

Security is a paramount concern in IaaS, and providers invest heavily in safeguarding their infrastructure and customer data. Encryption, access controls, and identity management are integral to ensuring the confidentiality and integrity of data. Compliance certifications and audit trails provide transparency and assurance to users that security and regulatory standards are met.

Despite its numerous advantages, IaaS is not without its challenges and considerations. Users must carefully plan and manage their infrastructure to control costs effectively. Without proper monitoring and governance, cloud expenses can escalate rapidly. Moreover, data privacy and compliance requirements must be addressed diligently, especially in industries subject to stringent regulations.

Vendor lock-in is another potential concern, as migrating infrastructure from one IaaS provider to another can be complex and costly. To mitigate this risk, organizations often adopt multi-cloud strategies, leveraging multiple providers to achieve flexibility and redundancy. Containers and container orchestration platforms like Kubernetes have also emerged as solutions to enhance portability across cloud environments.

In summary, Infrastructure as a Service (IaaS) represents a transformative paradigm in the realm of IT infrastructure management. It offers organizations a flexible, scalable, and cost-effective alternative to traditional on-premises hardware. By abstracting and virtualizing the underlying infrastructure, IaaS empowers users to provision, manage, and scale their resources with unprecedented ease. The self-service model, resource pooling, and a rich set of services make IaaS an attractive choice for businesses seeking to leverage the cloud for their computing needs. However, organizations must also navigate challenges such as cost management, security, and vendor lock-in as they embrace the benefits of IaaS. Ultimately, IaaS serves as a foundational building block in the cloud computing ecosystem, enabling innovation and agility in a rapidly evolving technological landscape.

Infrastructure as a Service (IaaS) comprises several fundamental components that collectively enable users to access and manage virtualized computing resources over the internet. These components form the building blocks of IaaS offerings, and understanding their roles and functionalities is essential for effectively harnessing the power of cloud infrastructure.

Virtual Machines (VMs): At the heart of IaaS are virtual machines, which serve as the fundamental computing units. VMs are software-based representations of physical servers, allowing users to run operating systems and applications in isolated environments. They provide the processing power needed to execute tasks and host applications, and users can create, configure, and manage VMs based on their specific requirements.

Storage: Storage is a critical component of IaaS, providing users with the ability to store and manage data in the cloud. IaaS offers various types of storage solutions, including block storage, object storage, and file storage. Block storage is used for data volumes and is ideal for databases and applications requiring high-speed access to data. Object storage is suitable for scalable and durable file storage, making it ideal for data backup, content delivery, and multimedia content. File storage offers shared file systems that can be accessed concurrently by multiple users or instances.

Networking Services: Networking services in IaaS enable users to establish, configure, and manage network connectivity within their cloud environments. This includes creating virtual networks, subnets, and configuring security groups and firewall rules to control traffic. Load balancers and content delivery networks (CDNs) play a crucial role in distributing traffic efficiently, improving application availability, and enhancing user experiences.

Compute Resources: Compute resources in IaaS encompass the virtualized processing power, memory, and computing capacity that users can allocate to their virtual machines. Users can select from a range of predefined VM sizes or customize the configuration to meet specific application requirements. Scalability is a key feature, allowing users to scale compute resources vertically by adding more power to existing VMs or horizontally by deploying additional VM instances.

Identity and Access Management: Security is a paramount concern in IaaS, and identity and access management (IAM) services play a crucial role in ensuring the confidentiality and integrity of data. IAM services enable users to define and manage access controls, permissions, and authentication mechanisms. This ensures that only authorized users and applications can access resources and data within the IaaS environment.

Security and Compliance: IaaS providers invest heavily in security measures to protect their infrastructure and customer data. These security measures include encryption, data loss prevention, threat detection, and security monitoring. Compliance certifications and audit trails provide transparency and assurance to users that security and regulatory standards are met.

Orchestration and Automation: IaaS environments often offer orchestration and automation tools that allow users to define, manage, and automate workflows and deployment processes. These tools enable users to streamline the provisioning of resources, application deployment, and scaling based on predefined policies and triggers. Orchestration simplifies complex tasks and ensures consistency across environments.

Monitoring and Management Tools: IaaS providers offer monitoring and management tools that empower users to gain insights into the performance, availability, and health of their infrastructure and applications. These tools provide real-time data, alerts, and dashboards, enabling users to proactively identify and address issues, optimize resource utilization, and meet service-level agreements (SLAs).

Cost Management and Billing: Effective cost management is crucial in IaaS environments, and providers offer tools to help users monitor and control their cloud spending. Users can analyze usage patterns, set budgets, and implement cost allocation strategies. Billing systems provide transparency by detailing usage and charges, allowing organizations to optimize resource utilization and control expenses.

API and Integration: IaaS environments expose APIs (Application Programming Interfaces) that enable developers to integrate and extend cloud services. APIs facilitate the automation of infrastructure provisioning, configuration, and management, enabling the development of cloud-native applications and seamless integration with other cloud services and third-party tools.

Backup and Disaster Recovery: Data protection is a critical consideration, and IaaS providers offer backup and disaster recovery solutions. Users can schedule automated backups, replicate data to different regions or data centers, and implement disaster recovery plans to ensure data availability and business continuity in case of unforeseen events.

Support and Service Level Agreements (SLAs): IaaS providers offer support options and SLAs that define the level of service and support users can expect. These agreements outline availability guarantees, response times for support requests, and escalation procedures. Users can choose the level of support that aligns with their specific needs and business requirements.

In summary, these key components collectively form the foundation of Infrastructure as a Service (IaaS) and provide the necessary building blocks for users to create, deploy, and manage their virtualized infrastructure and applications in the cloud. Understanding the roles and functionalities of these components is essential for effectively leveraging IaaS to meet business objectives, optimize resource utilization, and ensure a secure and efficient cloud environment.

Chapter 3: Benefits and Use Cases of IaaS

The adoption of Infrastructure as a Service (IaaS) brings a multitude of advantages and benefits to organizations of all sizes and industries. Understanding these advantages is essential for decision-makers and IT professionals looking to harness the power of IaaS to enhance their infrastructure and operations.

One of the primary advantages of IaaS is cost savings, as it eliminates the need for organizations to invest in and maintain physical hardware and data centers. This shift from a capital-intensive model to an operational expenditure model allows organizations to allocate resources more efficiently and reduce upfront infrastructure costs.

Scalability is another significant advantage of IaaS, as it enables organizations to scale their infrastructure up or down rapidly to accommodate changing workloads and demands. This scalability ensures that organizations can handle traffic spikes, accommodate growth, and optimize resource utilization without the need for lengthy procurement cycles.

IaaS provides flexibility and agility, allowing organizations to respond quickly to changing business requirements and market dynamics. Users can provision and manage resources independently through self-service portals, reducing reliance on IT departments and enabling faster development and deployment of applications.

Resource pooling is a core feature of IaaS, where computing resources are shared and allocated dynamically to multiple users in a multi-tenant environment. This efficient utilization of resources minimizes waste and results in cost savings for both providers and users.

High availability and reliability are inherent advantages of IaaS, as cloud providers invest heavily in redundant infrastructure, failover mechanisms, and data replication to ensure uninterrupted service availability. This ensures that critical applications and services remain accessible, even in the face of hardware failures or data center outages.

IaaS offers a rich ecosystem of services and components that enable users to build and customize their infrastructure environments. Users can select from a catalog of virtual machines, storage options, and networking services to match their specific application requirements, eliminating the constraints of physical hardware.

Security and compliance are paramount in IaaS, and providers invest heavily in security measures such as encryption, access controls, and threat detection to protect their infrastructure and customer data. Compliance certifications and attestations provide assurance to users that security and regulatory standards are met.

The self-service aspect of IaaS empowers users to provision and manage their infrastructure resources independently, reducing the time and effort required for resource allocation. This self-service model fosters innovation and agility within organizations, enabling development and operations teams to experiment, deploy, and scale applications more rapidly.

Disaster recovery and business continuity are simplified in IaaS environments, as users can replicate data to different regions or data centers and implement disaster recovery plans to ensure data availability and continuity in case of unforeseen events.

IaaS providers offer monitoring and management tools that provide real-time insights into the performance, availability, and health of infrastructure and applications. These tools enable users to proactively identify and address issues, optimize resource utilization, and meet service-level agreements (SLAs).

Cost management and billing tools empower users to monitor and control their cloud spending. Organizations can analyze usage patterns, set budgets, and implement cost allocation strategies to optimize resource utilization and control expenses.

Integration and interoperability are facilitated through APIs (Application Programming Interfaces) that enable developers to integrate and extend cloud services, automate infrastructure provisioning, and seamlessly connect with other cloud services and third-party tools.

Serverless computing, an emerging paradigm in IaaS, allows users to build and run applications without managing servers, reducing operational overhead and enabling more efficient use of resources.

Edge computing extends cloud capabilities to the edge of the network, reducing latency and enabling real-time processing for applications in areas such as the Internet of Things (IoT) and autonomous vehicles.

In summary, the adoption of Infrastructure as a Service (IaaS) offers numerous advantages, including cost savings, scalability, flexibility, high availability, and security. IaaS empowers organizations to respond quickly to changing business needs, streamline resource provisioning, and enhance innovation and agility. The rich ecosystem of services, self-service capabilities, and robust monitoring tools make IaaS a compelling choice for organizations seeking to optimize their infrastructure and operations in the cloud.

Infrastructure as a Service (IaaS) has found widespread adoption across various industries, revolutionizing the way organizations manage their IT infrastructure and applications. The real-world applications of IaaS are diverse and span a multitude of use cases, demonstrating its versatility and value in modern business operations.

One of the primary real-world applications of IaaS is web hosting and website management. Organizations can leverage IaaS to host websites and web applications, ensuring reliable and scalable access to online content. IaaS providers offer virtual machines, storage, and networking resources that enable organizations to deploy, manage, and scale their web presence effortlessly.

E-commerce platforms often rely on IaaS to support their online stores. IaaS allows e-commerce businesses to handle surges in website traffic during peak shopping seasons while maintaining the flexibility to scale resources up or down based on demand. This scalability ensures that online shoppers have a seamless and responsive shopping experience.

Software development and testing are another area where IaaS plays a pivotal role. Development teams can provision virtual development environments, replicate production configurations, and test software applications in controlled settings. IaaS offers the agility and flexibility needed to accelerate the development lifecycle and ensure the quality of software products.

Big Data and analytics applications benefit significantly from IaaS resources. Organizations can leverage IaaS to provision compute and storage resources to process and analyze vast datasets. This capability enables data scientists and analysts to gain insights and make data-driven decisions, facilitating innovation and competitive advantage.

Content delivery and media streaming services rely on IaaS to deliver digital content efficiently. IaaS providers offer content delivery networks (CDNs) that distribute content to geographically dispersed users, reducing latency and enhancing the user experience. Media companies can leverage IaaS to stream video and audio content reliably to global audiences.

IoT (Internet of Things) applications leverage IaaS for data processing and analysis at the edge of the network. Edge computing capabilities in IaaS enable IoT devices to process data locally, reducing latency and enabling real-time responses. This is critical for applications such as smart cities, autonomous vehicles, and industrial automation.

High-performance computing (HPC) applications in fields like scientific research, engineering simulations, and financial modeling benefit from the compute power and scalability of IaaS. Researchers and analysts can access IaaS resources to perform complex calculations and simulations, accelerating scientific discoveries and business insights.

Gaming companies use IaaS to power online gaming platforms and multiplayer experiences. IaaS provides the infrastructure needed to host game servers, manage player sessions, and ensure low-latency gameplay. This results in immersive gaming experiences and a competitive edge in the gaming industry.

Healthcare organizations leverage IaaS for secure and compliant healthcare IT solutions. IaaS providers offer HIPAA-compliant infrastructure and data protection measures, enabling healthcare providers to store and process patient data securely in the cloud. Telemedicine services also benefit from the scalability and accessibility of IaaS.

Financial services firms utilize IaaS for risk modeling, algorithmic trading, and financial analysis. IaaS resources provide the computational power required to process vast volumes of financial data and execute high-frequency trading strategies. Additionally, IaaS enables financial institutions to meet regulatory compliance requirements.

Educational institutions turn to IaaS for e-learning platforms and distance education. IaaS offers the infrastructure and scalability needed to support online courses, video lectures, and virtual classrooms. This enables students and educators to access educational resources from anywhere, fostering learning opportunities.

Non-profit organizations and government agencies utilize IaaS to support their missions and initiatives. IaaS allows these organizations to access cost-effective infrastructure resources, scale their operations as needed, and deploy applications for disaster recovery, public services, and data analysis.

Startups and small businesses benefit from IaaS as it provides an affordable and scalable infrastructure foundation. IaaS eliminates the need for significant upfront hardware investments, allowing startups to focus on innovation and growth without the burden of managing physical infrastructure.

In summary, the real-world applications of Infrastructure as a Service (IaaS) are vast and varied, encompassing web hosting, e-commerce, software development, Big Data analytics, content delivery, IoT, high-performance computing, gaming, healthcare, finance, education, non-profits, government, and startups. IaaS empowers organizations across industries to leverage scalable and cost-effective infrastructure resources, enabling innovation, agility, and competitive advantage in today's digital landscape.

Chapter 4: Key Players in the IaaS Market

In the world of cloud computing, several leading Infrastructure as a Service (IaaS) providers have emerged, offering a wide range of services and solutions to businesses and organizations worldwide. These providers have built robust and scalable cloud infrastructures that enable users to leverage virtualized computing resources, storage, and networking on-demand. Each of these leading IaaS providers has its own unique strengths and offerings, catering to diverse customer needs and requirements.

Amazon Web Services (AWS), often referred to as the pioneer of cloud computing, is a dominant player in the IaaS market. AWS boasts a comprehensive suite of cloud services, including virtual machines (EC2), scalable storage (S3), managed databases (RDS), and advanced machine learning tools (SageMaker). With a global network of data centers, AWS provides low-latency access to resources, making it a preferred choice for businesses of all sizes.

Microsoft Azure is Microsoft's cloud computing platform and one of the largest IaaS providers globally. Azure offers a broad array of services, including virtual machines (VMs), managed Kubernetes (AKS), and Azure Functions for serverless computing. Azure's integration with Windows-based environments and Microsoft products like Office 365 makes it particularly attractive to enterprises seeking hybrid cloud solutions.

Google Cloud Platform (GCP) is known for its expertise in data analytics and machine learning. GCP offers a wide range of IaaS services, such as Compute Engine for VMs, Kubernetes Engine for container orchestration, and Bigtable for NoSQL databases. Google's global network infrastructure provides fast and reliable access to cloud resources, making GCP a top choice for data-intensive workloads.

IBM Cloud is IBM's cloud computing offering, known for its enterprise-grade services and focus on hybrid and multicloud solutions. IBM Cloud provides virtual servers, managed Kubernetes (Red Hat OpenShift), and an extensive catalog of AI and blockchain services. With a strong emphasis on security and compliance, IBM Cloud is popular among organizations in regulated industries.

Oracle Cloud Infrastructure (OCI) is Oracle's IaaS platform, catering to enterprises that rely on Oracle databases and applications. OCI offers high-performance compute, block storage, and a range of Oracle-specific services, including Autonomous Database and Exadata Cloud Service. It is designed to deliver predictable performance and scalability for mission-critical workloads.

Alibaba Cloud, part of the Alibaba Group, is a dominant IaaS provider in the Asia-Pacific region and expanding globally. Alibaba Cloud offers a wide range of cloud services, including Elastic Compute Service (ECS), object storage (Object Storage Service), and a global content delivery network (CDN). Its strong presence in Asia makes it a preferred choice for businesses looking to expand in the region.

Tencent Cloud is one of the leading IaaS providers in China and has been expanding its global presence. Tencent Cloud offers virtual machines, cloud databases, and AI services. It is known for its strong focus on gaming and entertainment industries, providing infrastructure for online gaming and media streaming.

DigitalOcean is a cloud provider that targets developers and small to medium-sized businesses with its straightforward and developer-friendly offerings. DigitalOcean specializes in simplicity, offering virtual machines (Droplets), managed databases, and Kubernetes-based container orchestration (Kubernetes Service). It has gained popularity among startups and developers for its ease of use.

Salesforce is renowned for its customer relationship management (CRM) software but also offers its cloud infrastructure platform called Salesforce Platform. It provides scalable computing resources and services for building and deploying applications. Salesforce's strengths lie in its integration with CRM and business-focused applications.

Rackspace Technology, while not a traditional hyperscale cloud provider, is a managed cloud services company that helps businesses navigate and manage their cloud journey. Rackspace offers expertise across various cloud platforms, including AWS, Azure, Google Cloud, and more. It provides services such as cloud migration, optimization, and managed support.

These leading IaaS providers have carved out their niches in the cloud computing market, offering a diverse array of services and solutions to meet the needs of businesses, enterprises, developers, and organizations of all sizes. While each provider has its unique strengths and focus areas, the competition in the IaaS space continues to drive innovation, resulting in an ever-expanding set of features and capabilities for cloud users to leverage. As organizations evaluate their cloud strategy, they often consider factors such as specific use cases, geographic reach, compliance requirements, and integration with existing technologies when selecting the most suitable IaaS provider for their needs.

The competitive landscape in the Infrastructure as a Service (IaaS) industry is dynamic and constantly evolving, driven by the increasing demand for cloud services and the emergence of new players in the market. IaaS providers compete on several fronts, including pricing, service offerings, global reach, and specialization, as they vie for the attention and business of organizations seeking to harness the benefits of cloud infrastructure.

At the forefront of the IaaS industry are the major hyperscale cloud providers, including Amazon Web Services (AWS), Microsoft Azure, Google Cloud Platform (GCP), and IBM Cloud. These global giants have invested heavily in building vast data center infrastructures, spanning multiple regions around the world, to deliver scalable and reliable cloud services to a diverse customer base.

AWS, as the market leader, maintains a competitive edge by continually expanding its service portfolio, enhancing its infrastructure, and reducing costs through economies of scale. With a vast array of services, AWS appeals to a wide range of businesses, from startups to enterprises, and across various industries. Its relentless innovation and commitment to customer-centric solutions have solidified its position as a leader in the IaaS market.

Microsoft Azure, with its strong enterprise focus and deep integration with Windows-based environments, competes effectively for organizations looking to extend their existing Microsoft investments into the cloud. Azure's hybrid cloud capabilities, including Azure Stack, enable seamless integration between on-premises and cloud environments, making it an attractive choice for hybrid and multicloud strategies.

Google Cloud Platform (GCP) stands out for its expertise in data analytics, machine learning, and artificial intelligence. It appeals to businesses seeking advanced analytics solutions and offers a competitive advantage in data-intensive industries. GCP's global network infrastructure also ensures low-latency access to cloud resources, enhancing performance for global applications.

IBM Cloud differentiates itself by targeting enterprises with its focus on hybrid and multicloud solutions. It offers a suite of services, including AI-powered automation, blockchain, and managed services for IBM software products. IBM's emphasis on security and compliance positions it favorably in regulated industries, such as finance and healthcare.

Alibaba Cloud, while dominant in the Asia-Pacific region, competes globally with its extensive cloud services portfolio and a strong presence in emerging markets. Its competitive pricing and localization efforts make it a formidable player for businesses looking to expand in Asia.

Tencent Cloud, rooted in China, is gaining international recognition for its cloud offerings, particularly in gaming and entertainment. Its global expansion efforts target businesses with a focus on the Asian market and a need for reliable cloud infrastructure.

Oracle Cloud Infrastructure (OCI) caters to organizations relying on Oracle databases and applications, offering high-performance compute and storage services specifically designed for Oracle workloads. OCI's emphasis on predictable performance and reliability aligns with the needs of enterprises running mission-critical applications.

In addition to these major players, numerous regional and specialized IaaS providers compete by offering niche services and expertise. These providers often excel in specific industries or verticals, providing tailored solutions and local support.

DigitalOcean, for instance, appeals to developers and startups with its user-friendly platform and simplified pricing model. Its developer-centric approach has earned it a loyal customer base seeking straightforward and cost-effective cloud services.

Salesforce Platform, while primarily known for its CRM software, extends its reach into the IaaS market, focusing on cloud infrastructure and application development. Its strengths lie in its tight integration with Salesforce's suite of business applications.

Rackspace Technology, a managed cloud services provider, competes by offering expertise across multiple cloud platforms. It specializes in cloud management, migration, and optimization, helping businesses navigate the complexities of cloud adoption.

The competitive landscape in the IaaS industry also includes smaller, innovative startups that bring new ideas and technologies to the market. These startups often specialize in emerging areas such as serverless computing, edge computing, and container orchestration, contributing to the diversification of IaaS offerings.

As competition intensifies, IaaS providers differentiate themselves not only through technology but also through partnerships, ecosystem development, and customer support. Strategic alliances with software vendors, system integrators, and industry-specific solution providers enable IaaS providers to offer comprehensive solutions and capture a larger share of the market.

The IaaS industry is marked by ongoing price wars, with providers regularly reducing prices and offering discounts to attract customers. This competitive pricing benefits organizations as they can negotiate favorable terms and select the most cost-effective solutions.

In summary, the competitive landscape in the IaaS industry is marked by a dynamic interplay of global giants, regional players, specialized providers, and innovative startups. Organizations evaluating IaaS solutions must consider factors such as their specific use cases, geographic reach, compliance requirements, and integration with existing technologies when selecting the most suitable provider for their cloud infrastructure needs. This competitive environment drives innovation, expands service offerings, and ultimately benefits customers by providing a wide range of choices and options in the rapidly evolving world of cloud computing.

Chapter 5: Getting Started with AWS: Amazon Web Services

Amazon Web Services (AWS) is a comprehensive cloud computing platform that offers a vast array of services and solutions to organizations, ranging from startups to large enterprises. As one of the pioneers in cloud computing, AWS has played a significant role in transforming the IT landscape by providing on-demand access to a wide range of infrastructure and application services.

At its core, AWS is designed to deliver cloud resources as services, allowing organizations to offload the management and maintenance of physical infrastructure and instead focus on building, deploying, and scaling their applications and services. This shift from traditional on-premises infrastructure to cloud-based services has fundamentally changed the way businesses operate and innovate.

AWS is known for its global reach, with a network of data centers, known as Availability Zones, strategically located around the world. This global infrastructure ensures low-latency access to AWS services and enables businesses to deploy their applications in multiple regions to enhance performance, redundancy, and disaster recovery.

The AWS service portfolio covers a wide spectrum of computing, storage, networking, security, and management capabilities. These services are designed to address a diverse set of use cases, allowing organizations to tailor their cloud solutions to their specific needs.

Amazon Elastic Compute Cloud (EC2) is one of the foundational services of AWS, offering resizable virtual machines known as instances. EC2 provides flexibility and scalability for running applications, from small web servers to large, high-performance computing clusters. Users can choose from a variety of instance types optimized for different workloads.

Amazon Simple Storage Service (S3) is AWS's object storage service, designed for scalable and durable data storage. S3 is commonly used for storing and retrieving data, hosting static websites, and serving as a reliable backup and archival solution. It provides multiple storage classes to optimize costs based on data access patterns.

AWS Lambda is a serverless compute service that allows developers to run code without managing servers. With Lambda, organizations can execute code in response to events, such as changes in data, user actions, or API requests. This event-driven architecture simplifies application development and reduces operational overhead.

Amazon RDS (Relational Database Service) offers managed database services for popular database engines like MySQL, PostgreSQL, Oracle, and Microsoft SQL Server. RDS automates database administration tasks, such as backups, patch management, and scaling, allowing organizations to focus on application development.

Amazon VPC (Virtual Private Cloud) provides network isolation and control in the AWS cloud environment. Organizations can create isolated virtual networks, define subnets, configure routing, and establish secure connections to on-premises networks. VPC enables organizations to design and manage their network infrastructure in the cloud.

AWS Identity and Access Management (IAM) is a service that enables fine-grained control over user access and permissions to AWS resources. IAM allows organizations to create and manage user identities, roles, and policies to ensure security and compliance with least privilege principles.

Amazon CloudWatch is AWS's monitoring and observability service, providing insights into the performance and health of AWS resources and applications. CloudWatch collects and analyzes logs and metrics, triggers alarms, and allows organizations to visualize data through dashboards.

Amazon Elastic Container Service (ECS) and Amazon Elastic Kubernetes Service (EKS) are container orchestration services that simplify the deployment and management of containerized applications. These services support popular container platforms like Docker and Kubernetes, allowing organizations to scale and manage container workloads effectively.

AWS offers a rich ecosystem of artificial intelligence (AI) and machine learning (ML) services, including Amazon SageMaker for building, training, and deploying ML models, and Amazon Rekognition for image and video analysis. These services empower organizations to incorporate AI and ML capabilities into their applications.

Amazon Elastic Beanstalk is a platform-as-a-service (PaaS) offering that simplifies the deployment and management of web applications. With Elastic Beanstalk, developers can upload code, and AWS handles the provisioning, scaling, and monitoring of the underlying infrastructure.

AWS provides a wide range of security services and features to help organizations protect their data and applications. These include AWS Identity and Access Management (IAM), AWS Key Management Service (KMS) for data encryption, AWS Shield for DDoS protection, and AWS WAF (Web Application Firewall) for application security.

Amazon CloudFront is a content delivery network (CDN) service that accelerates the delivery of web content to users around the world. CloudFront improves website and application performance by caching and delivering content from edge locations close to the end-users.

AWS Direct Connect offers dedicated network connections between an organization's on-premises data centers and

AWS. This service provides private and reliable network connectivity, bypassing the public internet and ensuring low-latency access to AWS resources.

Amazon Aurora is a high-performance relational database engine compatible with MySQL and PostgreSQL. Aurora provides the performance and availability of commercial-grade databases while offering the cost-effectiveness and scalability of open-source databases.

AWS Marketplace is a digital catalog of third-party software and services that can be easily deployed on AWS. Organizations can discover, purchase, and deploy software solutions directly from the AWS Marketplace, simplifying software procurement and integration.

AWS offers a wide range of industry-specific solutions and services, including AWS GovCloud for government agencies, AWS for Healthcare for healthcare providers and organizations, and AWS for Financial Services for financial institutions.

In summary, AWS is a comprehensive cloud platform that empowers organizations to leverage a wide array of services and solutions to innovate, scale, and transform their operations. With its global reach, scalability, and rich service portfolio, AWS continues to be a leading choice for businesses looking to harness the benefits of cloud computing and drive digital transformation. Whether organizations are seeking to host web applications, process big data, or deploy machine learning models, AWS offers the tools and infrastructure to meet their diverse needs and challenges in the ever-evolving world of technology.

Setting up an Amazon Web Services (AWS) account is the first step in your journey to harness the power of cloud computing for your organization. Whether you're a startup looking to launch a new application or an enterprise seeking to migrate existing workloads to the cloud, creating an AWS account is a straightforward process that sets the foundation for your cloud infrastructure.

To begin, you'll need to visit the AWS website and navigate to the AWS Management Console, where you'll initiate the account creation process. Keep in mind that AWS accounts are billed on a pay-as-you-go basis, meaning you'll only pay for the resources you use, so you'll need to provide billing information during the account setup.

The first step in creating your AWS account is to provide your email address and choose a password. This email address will serve as your AWS account's root user, which has full access to all AWS services and resources, so it's essential to select a secure and easily accessible email address.

Once you've provided your email address and password, AWS will prompt you to enter some basic information, including your name and contact details. This information is used for account verification and billing purposes, so accuracy is crucial.

Next, you'll be asked to enter your phone number, which AWS may use for security and account recovery purposes. You'll receive a verification code via SMS or phone call to confirm your phone number.

After verifying your phone number, you'll need to provide a valid payment method for your AWS account. AWS accepts various payment options, including credit cards and bank accounts, depending on your location. It's essential to ensure that your payment method has sufficient funds or credit to cover potential charges.

AWS may charge a small, temporary authorization fee to validate your payment method, but this fee is typically reversed within a few days. Once your payment method is verified, your AWS account is officially created, and you gain access to the AWS Management Console.

As part of the account setup process, AWS will also ask you to choose a support plan. AWS offers various support plans, including Basic, Developer, Business, and Enterprise, each with different levels of support and access to AWS resources. The support plan you choose depends on your organization's needs and budget.

It's important to review the terms of the support plan carefully, as it outlines the service level agreements (SLAs) and response times you can expect from AWS support. Selecting an appropriate support plan ensures that you have access to technical assistance and resources when needed.

With your AWS account created and your support plan chosen, you can start exploring the AWS Management Console. The console is a web-based interface that allows you to manage and configure AWS services and resources, such as virtual machines, storage, databases, and networking.

Navigating the AWS Management Console may seem daunting at first due to the vast array of services and options available, but AWS provides extensive documentation, tutorials, and guides to help you get started. Additionally, AWS offers a free tier with limited usage of many services, allowing you to experiment and learn without incurring charges.

To enhance security and control over your AWS account, it's recommended to set up multi-factor authentication (MFA). MFA adds an extra layer of protection by requiring a second form of verification, typically a temporary code generated by a mobile app or hardware token, in addition to your password when logging in.

Enabling MFA for your root user account and for IAM (Identity and Access Management) users is a best practice to prevent unauthorized access to your AWS resources. AWS provides detailed instructions on setting up MFA for your account.

As you begin to use AWS services and deploy resources, it's essential to implement security best practices, such as configuring security groups and network access controls, encrypting data, and regularly reviewing and updating your security settings. AWS provides a range of security tools and services to help you protect your cloud environment.

In addition to security, managing costs and monitoring resource usage is crucial when using AWS. AWS offers cost management tools, such as AWS Cost Explorer and AWS Budgets, to help you track and optimize your spending. Setting up budgets and alerts can prevent unexpected charges and help you stay within your budget.

To gain visibility into your AWS resources' performance and health, you can use Amazon CloudWatch, a monitoring and observability service that collects and tracks metrics, collects and monitors log files, and sets alarms. CloudWatch allows you to monitor the operational health of your applications and gain insights into resource utilization.

As your organization's usage of AWS grows, you may consider creating AWS Identity and Access Management (IAM) users and roles to grant specific permissions to different individuals or services within your organization. IAM provides fine-grained control over who can access AWS resources and what actions they can perform.

IAM allows you to create policies that define permissions and attach them to users or roles. By implementing the principle of least privilege, you can ensure that users and services have only the permissions necessary to perform their tasks, reducing the risk of unauthorized access or accidental misconfigurations.

In summary, setting up your AWS account is the first step in harnessing the capabilities of cloud computing for your organization. It involves creating an AWS account, providing billing information, choosing a support plan, enabling security measures like MFA, and implementing best practices for security, cost management, and resource monitoring. With a well-configured AWS account, you'll be well-prepared to leverage the full range of AWS services and build scalable and reliable cloud solutions to meet your business needs.

Chapter 6: Exploring GCE: Google Cloud Engine

Google Cloud is a powerful and versatile cloud computing platform that offers a wide range of services and solutions to cater to the needs of businesses, developers, and enterprises. It encompasses a diverse set of services spanning computing, storage, data analytics, machine learning, and more, allowing users to build, deploy, and scale applications and workloads in the cloud.

At the core of Google Cloud's offerings is Google Compute Engine, which provides scalable and customizable virtual machines (VMs) for running applications and workloads. Users can choose from various machine types optimized for different computing needs, ensuring flexibility and performance.

Google Cloud Storage is a robust object storage service designed for secure and scalable data storage. It offers multi-regional, regional, and nearline storage classes, allowing organizations to choose the appropriate storage tier based on data access patterns and cost considerations.

BigQuery is Google Cloud's fully managed, serverless data warehouse solution for analytics and business intelligence. It enables users to analyze large datasets quickly and easily with the power of Google's infrastructure, making it ideal for data-driven decision-making.

Google Cloud offers Kubernetes Engine, a managed Kubernetes service that simplifies container orchestration. Users can deploy, manage, and scale containerized applications using Kubernetes, benefiting from Google's expertise in container technology.

Google's expertise in machine learning and artificial intelligence (AI) is evident in its cloud offerings. Cloud AI Platform provides tools and services for building, training, and deploying machine learning models at scale. It supports popular machine learning frameworks like TensorFlow and scikit-learn.

AutoML is another Google Cloud service that allows users to create custom machine learning models without the need for deep expertise in machine learning. AutoML simplifies the process of building models for tasks such as image recognition, natural language processing, and structured data analysis.

Google Cloud Pub/Sub is a messaging service that facilitates real-time data streaming and event-driven computing. It enables organizations to build event-driven applications, process and analyze data in real time, and trigger actions based on events.

Cloud Functions is a serverless compute service that allows users to run code in response to events without managing servers. With Cloud Functions, developers can create event-driven applications and automate tasks with ease.

Firebase, a mobile and web application development platform, is part of Google Cloud. Firebase offers a range of services for building and managing applications, including real-time database, authentication, hosting, and cloud functions.

Google Cloud's data analytics capabilities extend to Bigtable, a scalable NoSQL database for large analytical and operational workloads. It is designed to handle high-throughput, low-latency data access and is suitable for applications that require rapid data retrieval.

Google Cloud offers Cloud Spanner, a globally distributed, horizontally scalable database service that combines the benefits of relational databases with the scalability and reliability of NoSQL databases. It is designed for mission-critical applications requiring strong consistency and high availability.

For data integration and analytics, Google Cloud provides Dataflow, a fully managed stream and batch data processing service. Dataflow simplifies the development of data pipelines and supports real-time data processing.

Cloud Storage Transfer Service helps organizations move data to Google Cloud by simplifying the transfer and migration of data from on-premises or other cloud storage systems to Google Cloud Storage.

Google Cloud's data warehousing solution, Bigtable, offers a fully managed, highly scalable, and cost-effective data warehouse service that allows organizations to analyze and visualize data for business insights.

Google Cloud offers Apigee, an API management platform that enables organizations to design, secure, deploy, and analyze APIs. Apigee helps organizations manage their API ecosystems and drive digital transformation.

For identity and access management, Google Cloud Identity and Access Management (IAM) provides fine-grained control over user and resource access permissions. IAM allows organizations to define roles and policies to enforce security and compliance.

Networking capabilities in Google Cloud include Virtual Private Cloud (VPC), which provides isolated and customizable networking environments for applications. VPC allows users to create and manage private networks with control over IP addressing.

Google Cloud Load Balancing offers load balancing services for distributing traffic across multiple instances and regions, ensuring high availability and fault tolerance for applications.

Google Cloud CDN (Content Delivery Network) accelerates the delivery of web content to users globally, reducing latency and enhancing user experiences for websites and applications.

For security and compliance, Google Cloud offers Cloud Security Command Center, which provides centralized visibility and management of security-related data across Google Cloud resources. It helps organizations detect and mitigate security threats.

Data Loss Prevention (DLP) in Google Cloud helps organizations prevent the accidental exposure of sensitive information by automatically scanning and classifying data to enforce data protection policies.

Google Cloud's robust ecosystem of partners and marketplace offerings allows users to discover and deploy third-party solutions and services that complement Google Cloud's capabilities.

In summary, Google Cloud offers a comprehensive suite of services and offerings that cater to a wide range of cloud computing needs. Whether you are developing applications, managing data, running analytics, or ensuring security and compliance, Google Cloud provides the tools and infrastructure to support your cloud journey. As organizations increasingly embrace cloud technology, Google Cloud remains a competitive and innovative choice for achieving scalability, agility, and efficiency in the digital era.

In the world of cloud computing, Google Cloud Engine (GCE) stands out as a robust and flexible Infrastructure as a Service (IaaS) platform that allows you to deploy and manage virtual machines (VMs) on Google's infrastructure. Getting started with GCE and creating your first instance is an exciting step toward harnessing the power of cloud computing for your projects and workloads.

Before you dive into creating your first GCE instance, it's essential to have a Google Cloud Platform (GCP) account in place. If you don't have one yet, you can sign up for a GCP account on the Google Cloud website, and Google often offers free credits to get you started, making it an excellent opportunity for exploration.

Once you have your GCP account set up and have logged in to the GCP Console, you'll be greeted by a clean and intuitive interface that allows you to manage various GCP services, including GCE. The first step in creating your GCE instance is to navigate to the "Compute Engine" section in the GCP Console, where you'll find all the tools and options needed to manage your virtual machines.

To create a new GCE instance, you'll click on the "Create" button, which will initiate the instance creation process. This process involves configuring various settings and parameters to define the specifications of your virtual machine.

One of the crucial decisions you'll make during this process is selecting the operating system for your GCE instance. GCE offers a variety of operating system images, including popular choices like Ubuntu, CentOS, Debian, and Windows Server, allowing you to choose the one that best suits your requirements.

After selecting the operating system, you'll need to choose the machine type for your GCE instance. GCE offers a range of predefined machine types, each with different CPU and memory configurations, allowing you to balance performance and cost based on your needs. You can also create custom machine types if none of the predefined options fit your requirements.

Next, you'll configure the boot disk for your GCE instance. You can choose the boot disk's size and type (standard or SSD) to meet your storage and performance needs. Additionally, you can attach additional data disks to your instance if you require more storage capacity.

Networking is a crucial aspect of GCE instance creation. You'll need to select or create a network and subnet for your instance, assign a static IP address if needed, and configure firewall rules to control incoming and outgoing traffic to and from your instance. These networking settings ensure that your GCE instance is properly connected and secured within your virtual network.

You'll also have the option to enable various advanced settings, such as configuring metadata, startup scripts, and service accounts for your GCE instance. Metadata allows you to provide custom key-value pairs that your instance can access, while startup scripts can automate tasks when the instance boots up.

Service accounts play a crucial role in GCE instances by providing them with identity and access management capabilities. You can assign specific roles and permissions to your instances through service accounts, ensuring that they have the necessary access to interact with other GCP services and resources.

Once you've configured all the necessary settings for your GCE instance, you can review and validate your choices before proceeding with the creation process. Google Cloud provides a helpful summary of your instance's configuration, allowing you to double check everything before deployment.

Once you're satisfied with the configuration, you can click the "Create" button to initiate the GCE instance creation process. Google Cloud will provision the virtual machine according to your specifications, which may take a few minutes.

Once your GCE instance is successfully created, you'll receive important information such as the instance's external IP address, which you can use to connect to the virtual machine over the internet. You can access your GCE instance through various methods, including SSH for Linux instances or Remote Desktop for Windows instances.

Managing and maintaining your GCE instance is made easy through the GCP Console and various command-line tools and APIs provided by Google Cloud. You can stop, start, resize, or even delete your instances as needed, allowing you to adapt to changing workloads and requirements.

Additionally, GCE instances can be part of managed instance groups, which provide features such as automatic scaling, load balancing, and rolling updates. These capabilities enable you to build highly available and resilient applications that can handle increased traffic and maintain high uptime.

Google Cloud also offers various monitoring and logging tools, such as Google Cloud Monitoring and Google Cloud Logging, to help you keep an eye on the performance and health of your GCE instances. You can set up alerts, create custom dashboards, and gain insights into resource utilization to ensure optimal operation.

In summary, creating your first GCE instance is a fundamental step in leveraging the capabilities of Google Cloud Engine for your cloud computing needs. With a user-friendly interface, flexible configuration options, and a wide selection of operating systems and machine types, GCE empowers you to deploy and manage virtual machines efficiently. As you explore and experiment with GCE instances, you'll discover the agility, scalability, and reliability that cloud computing can bring to your projects and applications.

Chapter 7: Microsoft Azure: Your Path to the Cloud

Microsoft Azure is a comprehensive cloud computing platform that offers a vast array of services and solutions designed to meet the diverse needs of organizations, developers, and businesses worldwide. As one of the leading cloud providers, Azure has established itself as a trusted platform for building, deploying, and managing applications and services in the cloud.

At the heart of the Azure ecosystem is Microsoft's commitment to providing a robust and secure cloud environment. Azure offers a wide range of services across various categories, including computing, storage, networking, databases, analytics, artificial intelligence (AI), and Internet of Things (IoT), empowering users to create innovative solutions and drive digital transformation.

Azure's computing services are centered around Azure Virtual Machines (VMs), which offer scalable and customizable compute resources that cater to diverse workloads and application requirements. Users can choose from a variety of VM sizes and configurations to match their specific needs, whether it's running web applications, hosting databases, or performing high-performance computing tasks.

Azure Functions, a serverless compute service, allows developers to build event-driven, serverless applications without the need to manage infrastructure. With Azure Functions, you can execute code in response to events such as HTTP requests, database changes, or messages from event hubs.

Azure Kubernetes Service (AKS) provides managed Kubernetes clusters that simplify container orchestration and management. AKS enables organizations to deploy, scale, and manage containerized applications efficiently, leveraging the power of Kubernetes without the operational overhead.

Azure App Service offers a fully managed platform for building, deploying, and scaling web and mobile applications. It supports popular programming languages, frameworks, and continuous integration and delivery (CI/CD) pipelines, streamlining application development and deployment.

Azure provides a range of managed database services, including Azure SQL Database, Azure Cosmos DB, and Azure Database for PostgreSQL, among others. These services offer high availability, automatic backups, and scaling capabilities, reducing the operational burden on database administrators.

Azure Storage offers scalable and reliable storage solutions for a variety of data types, including blobs, files, tables, and queues. Azure Blob Storage, in particular, is widely used for storing unstructured data, such as images, videos, and backups, while Azure Files provides fully managed file shares for cloud-native and hybrid scenarios.

Azure Networking services empower organizations to create secure and connected cloud environments. Azure Virtual Network (VNet) allows users to define private, isolated network segments with control over IP address ranges, subnets, and routing. Azure ExpressRoute provides dedicated private connections to Azure from on-premises data centers, ensuring secure and high-performance network connectivity.

Azure Load Balancer and Application Gateway offer load balancing and traffic management solutions to distribute incoming network traffic across multiple instances for improved availability and fault tolerance.

Azure Firewall and Azure DDoS Protection provide advanced security measures to safeguard cloud resources against threats and attacks. These services offer features such as application-level filtering, intrusion detection, and mitigation of distributed denial of service (DDoS) attacks.

Azure Active Directory (Azure AD) is Microsoft's identity and access management service, providing secure and seamless authentication and authorization for users and applications. Azure AD supports single sign-on (SSO), multi-factor authentication (MFA), and integration with thousands of popular applications.

Azure Key Vault is a centralized secrets management service that allows organizations to securely store and manage cryptographic keys, certificates, and other sensitive information. Key Vault helps ensure data protection and compliance with regulatory requirements.

Azure DevOps Services offers a suite of tools for software development, including version control, continuous integration, continuous delivery, and project management. It enables teams to collaborate and deliver software efficiently and with high quality.

Azure Monitor and Azure Security Center provide monitoring, logging, and security insights for Azure resources. Azure Monitor helps organizations gain visibility into resource performance and health, while Azure Security Center offers threat protection, vulnerability assessment, and security recommendations.

Azure Cognitive Services provides a suite of AI and machine learning capabilities, including vision, speech, language, and decision-making APIs. Developers can leverage these services to build intelligent applications that can see, hear, understand, and interact with users in natural ways.

Azure IoT services enable organizations to connect, monitor, and manage IoT devices and assets. Azure IoT Hub, Azure IoT Central, and Azure Sphere offer comprehensive solutions for IoT device management, data ingestion, and analytics.

Azure offers a rich ecosystem of tools, libraries, and integrations to enhance development and operations. Azure DevTest Labs, Azure Functions, Azure Logic Apps, and Azure API Management are just a few examples of services that streamline application development and automation.

Azure Marketplace is a curated marketplace of third-party applications and services that can be easily deployed on Azure. Organizations can discover, evaluate, and deploy solutions directly from the Azure Marketplace, accelerating application development and integration.

Azure also supports hybrid cloud scenarios, allowing organizations to seamlessly extend their on-premises data centers to the cloud. Azure Arc, for instance, enables organizations to manage and govern resources across on-premises, multi-cloud, and edge environments from a single control plane.

In summary, the Azure services and ecosystem offer a powerful and flexible platform for organizations seeking to leverage the benefits of cloud computing. With a wide range of services spanning computing, storage, networking, security, AI, and IoT, Azure provides the tools and infrastructure necessary to build, deploy, and scale applications and services in a secure and compliant manner. As organizations embark on their cloud journey, Azure remains a trusted and innovative partner in achieving their digital transformation goals.

In the realm of cloud computing, Microsoft Azure stands as a formidable platform that offers a wide array of services and solutions designed to meet the diverse needs of organizations and businesses. As a cloud provider, Azure has emerged as a trusted platform for building, deploying, and managing applications and services in the cloud. To embark on your journey with Azure, the first step is to establish your presence within the Azure ecosystem.

Setting up your Azure presence begins with creating an Azure account. If you don't already have one, you can easily sign up for an Azure account on the Microsoft Azure website. Azure often offers free credits to new users, making it an excellent opportunity for exploration and experimentation.

Once your Azure account is established, you gain access to the Azure Portal, a web-based interface that serves as your gateway to managing Azure resources and services. The portal offers a user-friendly environment with a dashboard that provides an overview of your Azure resources and services.

One of the core concepts in Azure is the Azure Resource Group, which acts as a logical container for organizing and managing related Azure resources. When you create resources, you typically place them within a resource group, simplifying resource management and lifecycle.

Creating your first Azure resource group is a fundamental step in organizing your Azure resources effectively. You can do this directly through the Azure Portal by selecting "Resource groups" and choosing "Create a resource group." Give it a meaningful name that reflects the purpose of the group.

With your resource group in place, you can start creating Azure resources within it. The Azure Marketplace is a valuable resource for discovering and deploying pre-configured applications and services. It offers a vast catalog of solutions, from virtual machines to databases to web applications.

Azure Virtual Machines (VMs) are a fundamental Azure resource that allows you to run Windows or Linux-based workloads in the cloud. To create your first Azure VM, you'll need to specify details such as the operating system, size, and network settings. Azure offers a variety of VM sizes, enabling you to balance performance and cost.

Azure App Service is another essential resource for hosting web applications and APIs. It simplifies application deployment by providing a fully managed platform for web hosting. With App Service, you can focus on coding your applications while Azure handles the infrastructure.

Azure Blob Storage is Azure's object storage service, designed for storing large amounts of unstructured data, such as documents, images, and backups. Creating a Blob Storage account within your resource group is a useful step for storing and managing your data.

Azure SQL Database is a managed relational database service that supports SQL Server workloads. It offers high availability, automatic backups, and scaling capabilities. Creating an Azure SQL Database instance allows you to store and manage structured data effectively.

Networking is a crucial aspect of your Azure presence. Azure Virtual Network (VNet) enables you to create isolated network segments, define subnets, and establish secure connections to on-premises networks. Setting up a VNet tailored to your organization's requirements is essential for network isolation and control.

Azure Security Center is a valuable tool for enhancing the security of your Azure resources. It provides recommendations and insights into security best practices, helping you protect your cloud environment from threats and vulnerabilities.

Azure Monitor and Azure Log Analytics offer comprehensive monitoring and insights into the performance and health of your Azure resources. These tools enable you to collect and analyze telemetry data, set up alerts, and gain visibility into your resource utilization.

Azure Identity and Access Management (IAM) is pivotal for controlling user access and permissions to Azure resources.

You can create custom roles and policies to ensure secure and least-privilege access.

As you build your Azure presence, it's essential to consider compliance and governance. Azure Policy allows you to enforce organizational standards and requirements across your resources. You can define policies that govern resource configurations and ensure compliance with regulatory standards.

Azure Blueprints is another tool for streamlining governance by providing a repeatable and standardized way to deploy environments. Blueprints allow you to define and enforce resource configurations, ensuring consistency across deployments.

Azure DevOps Services is a suite of tools that supports the entire software development lifecycle. It includes version control, continuous integration, continuous delivery, project management, and collaboration tools. Integrating Azure DevOps into your Azure presence streamlines application development and deployment.

Azure also offers a wide range of development tools, SDKs, and services for building applications and services. Whether you're developing with .NET, Python, Java, or other programming languages, Azure provides the resources and support you need.

Hybrid cloud scenarios are increasingly prevalent, and Azure offers solutions for seamlessly extending your on-premises data center to the cloud. Azure Arc allows you to manage and govern resources across on-premises, multi-cloud, and edge environments from a single control plane.

In summary, establishing your presence in Azure is the first step toward leveraging the capabilities of Microsoft's cloud platform. With a well-organized resource group, a selection of Azure resources, a secure network configuration, and compliance and governance measures in place, you're well-prepared to start building, deploying, and managing your applications and services in the cloud. As you explore Azure's capabilities and services, you'll discover the agility, scalability, and innovation that Azure brings to your digital transformation journey.

Chapter 8: IBM Cloud: A Comprehensive IaaS Solution

IBM Cloud, a robust and multifaceted cloud computing platform, offers a comprehensive suite of services and solutions tailored to meet the evolving needs of businesses and enterprises. As one of the prominent players in the cloud industry, IBM Cloud empowers organizations to innovate, modernize, and drive digital transformation through cloud-native applications, data analytics, and artificial intelligence (AI).

At the core of IBM Cloud's offerings is its commitment to providing a secure and scalable cloud environment. With a wide range of services spanning infrastructure, platform, and software, IBM Cloud caters to diverse workloads and use cases, enabling organizations to harness the full potential of cloud computing.

IBM Cloud's Infrastructure as a Service (IaaS) offerings encompass a spectrum of compute, storage, and networking solutions. IBM Virtual Servers provide flexible and scalable virtual machines (VMs) that cater to various workloads, from web applications to databases. Users can select from a variety of VM configurations to match their performance and resource requirements.

IBM Cloud Object Storage is designed for scalable, cost-effective, and durable data storage. It supports object, file, and block storage, making it suitable for a wide range of data types and access patterns. Data can be stored in different storage classes based on its frequency of access and retention requirements.

IBM Cloud Kubernetes Service simplifies container orchestration by providing managed Kubernetes clusters. It enables organizations to deploy, manage, and scale containerized applications seamlessly, leveraging the power of Kubernetes without the operational complexity.

IBM Cloud Functions is a serverless compute service that allows developers to run code in response to events without managing servers. With Cloud Functions, organizations can build event-driven applications and automate tasks efficiently.

For application development and deployment, IBM Cloud Foundry offers a platform as a service (PaaS) that simplifies the development and scaling of applications. Developers can focus on writing code while IBM Cloud Foundry manages the underlying infrastructure and services.

IBM Cloud Databases provide managed database services for various database engines, including PostgreSQL, MySQL, and Db2. These services offer high availability, automated backups, and scaling capabilities, simplifying database administration.

IBM Cloud Networking services enable organizations to create secure and connected cloud environments. IBM Cloud Virtual Private Cloud (VPC) allows users to define isolated network segments with full control over IP addressing, subnets, and routing.

IBM Cloud Internet Services offers a suite of network performance and security solutions, including content delivery, DDoS protection, and load balancing, to enhance application delivery and security.

Security is paramount in IBM Cloud, with services like IBM Cloud Security Advisor providing insights and recommendations for improving cloud security. IBM Cloud Identity and Access Management (IAM) allows organizations to control access to resources and enforce security policies.

IBM Cloud Key Protect is a centralized key management service that allows organizations to securely store, manage, and rotate cryptographic keys, ensuring data protection and compliance with regulations.

IBM Cloud offers a wide range of services for artificial intelligence and machine learning. IBM Watson provides AI and machine learning capabilities, including natural language understanding, computer vision, and language translation, to build intelligent applications.

IBM Watson Studio is a comprehensive platform for data science and machine learning, offering tools for data preparation, model development, and deployment. It streamlines the end-to-end process of building and deploying machine learning models.

IBM Cloud Pak for Data is an integrated data and AI platform that helps organizations collect, organize, and analyze data for actionable insights. It provides a unified environment for data scientists, data engineers, and business analysts to collaborate on data projects.

IBM Cloud for Financial Services is a cloud platform designed to meet the stringent regulatory and security requirements of the financial industry. It offers industry-specific services and controls to help financial institutions migrate to the cloud securely.

IBM Cloud Satellite extends the capabilities of IBM Cloud to on-premises and edge environments. Organizations can manage and deploy cloud services consistently across multiple locations, enabling hybrid cloud scenarios.

IBM Cloud Marketplace offers a curated selection of third-party solutions and services that complement IBM Cloud offerings. Users can discover, evaluate, and deploy these solutions to meet their specific business needs.

IBM Cloud for VMware Solutions provides a hybrid cloud solution for enterprises using VMware virtualization technologies. It allows organizations to seamlessly extend their on-premises VMware workloads to the cloud.

In summary, IBM Cloud offers a comprehensive ecosystem of services and solutions that empower organizations to innovate and transform digitally. With a broad range of services spanning infrastructure, platform, and AI, IBM Cloud provides the tools and infrastructure necessary to build, deploy, and scale applications and services securely and efficiently. As organizations navigate their cloud journey, IBM Cloud remains a trusted and innovative partner in achieving their digital transformation goals.

Provisioning resources in IBM Cloud is a pivotal step in harnessing the capabilities of this cloud computing platform, enabling organizations to build, deploy, and manage their applications and services in a flexible and scalable environment. Provisioning refers to the process of creating and configuring cloud resources, including virtual machines, storage, and networking, to support various workloads and use cases.

IBM Cloud offers a user-friendly and intuitive interface that facilitates resource provisioning. The IBM Cloud Console serves as the primary portal for managing and provisioning resources, providing users with a unified and streamlined experience. To get started with provisioning resources, users can access the IBM Cloud Console through a web browser and log in to their IBM Cloud account.

One of the fundamental concepts in provisioning resources is the IBM Cloud Region. Regions represent geographically dispersed data centers that house IBM Cloud resources. IBM Cloud offers a wide selection of regions across the globe, allowing users to choose the region that best aligns with their data residency and latency requirements.

When provisioning resources, selecting the appropriate region is a crucial decision. Users can choose a region closest to their target audience to minimize latency and optimize performance. Additionally, selecting the right region ensures compliance with data sovereignty regulations and helps achieve high availability and disaster recovery objectives.

Once users have selected their desired region, they can proceed with creating cloud resources within it. IBM Cloud Resource Groups provide a logical and organizational structure for grouping related resources. By organizing resources into resource groups, users can manage and monitor them collectively, simplifying resource management.

To create a resource group, users navigate to the IBM Cloud Console and access the "Resource groups" section. Within this section, they can create a new resource group and assign a meaningful name that reflects the purpose or project associated with the group. This resource group becomes the container for the cloud resources users intend to provision.

Virtual machines (VMs) are a foundational resource in cloud computing, and IBM Cloud offers a variety of VM configurations to cater to different workloads and performance requirements. Provisioning a VM involves specifying details such as the VM size, operating system, and networking settings.

IBM Cloud provides a wide range of pre-configured VM images for popular operating systems, including Linux and Windows. Users can select an image that aligns with their application's requirements and development preferences. Additionally, users can create custom images with specific software configurations and deploy VMs based on these custom images.

VM size selection is another critical aspect of VM provisioning. IBM Cloud offers a range of VM sizes, each with different CPU, memory, and storage configurations. Users can choose a VM size that matches their workload's resource demands while considering cost-efficiency.

Networking configuration plays a vital role in VM provisioning. IBM Cloud Virtual Private Cloud (VPC) allows users to create isolated network segments within their IBM Cloud environment. When provisioning VMs, users can assign VMs to specific subnets within their VPC, ensuring network isolation and control.

IBM Cloud Security Groups provide network security policies that control inbound and outbound traffic to and from VMs. Users can associate security groups with VMs to define firewall rules and restrict network access based on IP addresses and ports. This granular control enhances the security posture of provisioned resources.

Storage provisioning is another essential aspect of resource provisioning in IBM Cloud. IBM Cloud Block Storage allows users to create and attach additional block storage volumes to VMs to meet their storage capacity requirements. Block storage volumes can be dynamically attached and detached from VMs, offering flexibility and scalability.

IBM Cloud Object Storage is a scalable and cost-effective solution for storing unstructured data, such as images, videos, and backups. Users can create Object Storage buckets to organize and manage their data effectively. Object Storage provides different storage classes, allowing users to optimize costs based on data access patterns.

Networking is a critical consideration when provisioning resources in IBM Cloud. IBM Cloud Load Balancer offers load balancing services to distribute incoming traffic across multiple VM instances, ensuring high availability and fault tolerance for applications.

IBM Cloud Direct Link provides dedicated private network connections to IBM Cloud from on-premises data centers. This secure and high-speed connectivity option is valuable for enterprises seeking to integrate their on-premises infrastructure with IBM Cloud.

Security is a paramount concern in cloud provisioning. IBM Cloud Identity and Access Management (IAM) allows users to define access controls, roles, and permissions for their resources. IAM policies help enforce security and compliance requirements.

IBM Cloud Key Protect serves as a centralized key management service for securely storing and managing cryptographic keys used to encrypt and decrypt data. Key Protect helps organizations maintain data security and regulatory compliance.

Once users have provisioned their resources, they can manage and monitor them through the IBM Cloud Console and various command-line tools and APIs. Resource management encompasses tasks such as starting and stopping VMs, resizing storage volumes, and adjusting networking configurations.

IBM Cloud offers a range of monitoring and logging tools to provide insights into resource performance and health. Users can set up alerts, create custom dashboards, and analyze resource utilization to ensure optimal operation.

In summary, provisioning resources in IBM Cloud is a foundational step in leveraging the capabilities of this cloud platform. With a well-organized resource group, a selection of cloud resources, and appropriate network and security configurations, users are well-equipped to build, deploy, and manage their applications and services in a secure and efficient cloud environment. As organizations embark on their cloud journey, IBM Cloud remains a trusted partner in achieving scalability, agility, and innovation in the digital era.

Chapter 9: Managing IaaS Resources Effectively

Resource management in the context of cloud computing is a critical aspect of optimizing the use of cloud resources and ensuring cost-effectiveness. Effective resource management involves the allocation, monitoring, and optimization of cloud resources to meet application requirements efficiently. Next, we will explore best practices for resource management in the cloud.

One of the foundational best practices in resource management is to start with a well-defined cloud strategy. Organizations should establish clear objectives and goals for their cloud usage, taking into account factors such as scalability, performance, security, and cost. A well-defined strategy serves as a guiding framework for resource management decisions.

Resource tagging is a valuable practice for organizing and categorizing cloud resources. By applying tags to resources, organizations can easily track and manage them based on attributes such as application, environment, owner, or cost center. Tags provide visibility into resource ownership and usage.

Regularly reviewing and auditing cloud resources is essential for resource management. Organizations should periodically assess the utilization and performance of resources to identify underutilized or overprovisioned assets. This practice helps in making informed decisions about resource resizing or decommissioning.

Implementing an effective cost allocation and chargeback mechanism is crucial for resource management. By assigning costs to individual departments or teams based on their resource usage, organizations can promote accountability and control over cloud spending. This encourages teams to optimize their resource usage.

Resource monitoring and performance optimization are ongoing activities in cloud resource management. Organizations should implement monitoring solutions to track resource performance and detect anomalies or bottlenecks. Automated alerts and notifications can help in proactively addressing performance issues.

Implementing resource auto-scaling is a best practice for ensuring optimal resource utilization. Auto-scaling allows resources to automatically adjust to changing workloads, ensuring that organizations pay for resources only when they are needed. This practice improves cost efficiency.

Resource rightsizing involves periodically reviewing resource configurations to align them with actual usage patterns. Organizations should assess whether resources are over-provisioned or under-provisioned and make adjustments accordingly. Rightsizing helps in optimizing resource costs.

Leveraging cloud-native management tools and services is essential for effective resource management. Cloud providers offer a range of tools for resource monitoring, optimization, and automation. Organizations should leverage these tools to streamline resource management tasks.

Implementing resource policies and governance controls is critical for resource management in multi-cloud or hybrid cloud environments. Policies can enforce resource naming conventions, access controls, and compliance requirements. Governance controls help in maintaining resource consistency.

Resource tagging and metadata can enhance resource discovery and categorization. Organizations should document resource attributes, dependencies, and configurations using metadata. This information aids in resource management and troubleshooting.

Resource consolidation is a practice that involves combining multiple smaller resources into fewer, larger resources. Consolidation can lead to cost savings by reducing the number of resource instances to manage. However, organizations should carefully assess the impact on performance and availability.

Resource lifecycle management involves defining processes for resource provisioning, modification, and decommissioning. Organizations should establish clear workflows for resource requests and approvals to ensure that resources are provisioned and de-provisioned according to best practices.

Implementing resource access controls and security measures is paramount in resource management. Organizations should define access policies and permissions to prevent unauthorized access or modifications to resources. Security measures should include encryption, identity and access management, and threat detection.

Resource backup and disaster recovery strategies should be part of resource management planning. Organizations should regularly back up critical data and configurations and establish disaster recovery plans to minimize downtime in case of unforeseen events.

Resource documentation and documentation practices are essential for resource management. Organizations should maintain up-to-date documentation that includes resource configurations, dependencies, and operational procedures. Documentation aids in troubleshooting and resource management.

Resource forecasting and capacity planning are proactive practices in resource management. Organizations should analyze historical resource usage patterns and anticipate future resource needs. Capacity planning helps in avoiding resource shortages or over-provisioning.

Resource performance optimization involves fine-tuning resource configurations to achieve optimal performance. Organizations should periodically assess resource performance and make adjustments to settings such as CPU, memory, and storage to meet application requirements efficiently.

Resource cost optimization is a continuous effort in resource management. Organizations should regularly review cloud cost reports and usage data to identify cost-saving opportunities. Strategies for cost optimization may include reserved instances, spot instances, and cost monitoring tools.

Resource compliance and governance should align with organizational policies and industry regulations. Organizations should implement controls and monitoring to ensure that resources comply with security, privacy, and regulatory requirements. Compliance audits should be conducted regularly.

Resource management tools and automation solutions can streamline resource provisioning, monitoring, and optimization. Organizations should invest in tools that provide visibility into resource usage, automate resource scaling, and enforce governance policies.

Resource management practices should align with organizational goals and priorities. Organizations should regularly review and update resource management strategies to adapt to changing business needs and technology trends.

In summary, effective resource management is essential for optimizing the use of cloud resources, controlling costs, and ensuring the performance and security of applications and services. By following best practices such as resource tagging, monitoring, rightsizing, and cost optimization, organizations can achieve efficient resource management in the cloud.

Scaling and optimization are fundamental principles in cloud computing that enable organizations to adapt to changing workloads, control costs, and maximize the efficiency of their cloud resources. Next, we will explore various strategies and best practices for scaling and optimizing cloud resources.

One of the key strategies for scaling in the cloud is horizontal scaling, also known as "scaling out." Horizontal scaling involves adding more instances of resources, such as virtual machines (VMs) or containers, to distribute the workload and increase capacity. This strategy is particularly useful for applications with variable or unpredictable workloads.

Vertical scaling, on the other hand, involves increasing the capacity of existing resources by upgrading their specifications, such as CPU, memory, or storage. Vertical scaling is suitable for applications that require additional resources without adding more instances.

Auto-scaling is an automated scaling strategy that allows cloud resources to adapt to changing workloads automatically. With auto-scaling policies in place, resources can scale up or down based on predefined conditions, such as CPU utilization or incoming traffic. Auto-scaling helps organizations maintain performance and cost efficiency.

Load balancing is a crucial component of scaling strategies. Load balancers distribute incoming traffic across multiple instances to ensure even distribution of workloads and improve fault tolerance. Load balancers can be used for applications, databases, and other services to optimize resource utilization.

Content delivery networks (CDNs) are valuable for optimizing content delivery and improving latency for users across the globe. CDNs cache content in edge locations, reducing the distance and time it takes to retrieve content for users. This strategy enhances the performance and user experience.

Serverless computing is a cloud architecture that allows organizations to run code without managing servers. Serverless platforms, such as AWS Lambda, Azure Functions, or Google Cloud Functions, automatically scale resources based on incoming requests. This approach is ideal for event-driven and microservices architectures.

Resource utilization monitoring is essential for optimizing cloud resources. Organizations should regularly monitor the utilization of resources such as CPU, memory, and storage to identify underutilized or overprovisioned resources. Monitoring tools and dashboards provide insights into resource performance.

Rightsizing involves adjusting resource configurations to align them with actual usage patterns. Organizations should regularly review resource sizes and specifications and make adjustments to optimize cost and performance. Rightsizing can lead to cost savings by eliminating unnecessary resources.

Reserved instances or reserved capacity are cost-saving strategies offered by cloud providers. By committing to reserved instances for a predefined period, organizations can benefit from discounted pricing compared to on-demand resources. Reserved capacity is suitable for predictable workloads.

Spot instances or preemptible VMs are cost-effective options for workloads that can tolerate interruptions. These instances are available at significantly reduced prices compared to on-demand resources but may be terminated when the cloud provider needs the capacity for other customers.

Resource tagging and labeling are important for cost allocation and optimization. Tags and labels help organizations track resource ownership, project or department allocation, and cost attribution. They provide visibility into resource usage patterns.

Cost monitoring and budgeting are integral to optimization efforts. Organizations should set budgets and cost alerts to track spending and ensure that it aligns with financial goals. Cost monitoring tools and reports help organizations identify cost outliers and areas for optimization.

Resource optimization policies can be defined to enforce best practices and governance rules. Policies can control resource provisioning, enforce tagging standards, and restrict the creation of certain resource types. Governance policies help organizations maintain resource consistency.

Storage optimization involves managing and optimizing data storage costs. Organizations should regularly review data storage usage, archive or delete outdated data, and leverage storage tiering options to optimize costs while meeting data retention requirements.

Networking optimization strategies include optimizing data transfer costs by selecting the appropriate network tier and optimizing network routing to reduce latency and improve performance. Organizations should also consider implementing content delivery networks (CDNs) for content caching and delivery.

Database optimization involves optimizing database configurations, query performance, and storage costs. Organizations should regularly review database usage, implement indexing and caching strategies, and leverage managed database services to reduce administrative overhead.

Resource decommissioning is an essential part of optimization. Organizations should establish processes for decommissioning resources that are no longer needed or have become obsolete. Decommissioning helps reduce costs and maintain resource hygiene.

Cloud cost management tools and platforms can assist organizations in optimizing costs and resource utilization. These tools provide visibility into cost breakdowns, spending trends, and cost optimization recommendations. Organizations can leverage these insights to make informed decisions.

In summary, scaling and optimization are essential practices in cloud resource management. Organizations can achieve efficiency, cost savings, and improved performance by implementing strategies such as horizontal scaling, auto-scaling, load balancing, and cost monitoring. Continuous monitoring, rightsizing, and cost allocation practices ensure that cloud resources align with business objectives while controlling costs effectively. By embracing these strategies and best practices, organizations can harness the full potential of cloud computing while maintaining cost-effectiveness.

Chapter 10: Best Practices and Future Trends in IaaS

In the realm of Infrastructure as a Service (IaaS), security and performance are paramount concerns for organizations seeking to harness the power of cloud computing while safeguarding their data and applications. As organizations migrate their infrastructure to the cloud, it is crucial to adopt best practices that address these concerns comprehensively.

One of the foundational best practices for IaaS security is to establish a robust identity and access management (IAM) strategy. IAM enables organizations to control who can access their cloud resources and what actions they can perform. It involves the management of user identities, roles, and permissions to ensure that only authorized users have access to sensitive resources.

Implementing strong authentication mechanisms, such as multi-factor authentication (MFA), adds an extra layer of security by requiring users to provide multiple forms of verification before gaining access to cloud resources. MFA helps prevent unauthorized access, even in the event of stolen credentials.

Encryption is a fundamental security measure for protecting data in transit and at rest within IaaS environments. Organizations should implement encryption protocols, such as Transport Layer Security (TLS) for data in transit and encryption at the storage layer for data at rest. Encryption keys should be managed securely using key management services.

Regularly auditing and monitoring cloud resources is a critical aspect of IaaS security. Organizations should use cloud-native monitoring and auditing tools to track user activities, resource changes, and security events. Automated alerts and notifications should be set up to detect and respond to security incidents promptly.

Implementing network security controls is essential for securing IaaS environments. Organizations should configure firewalls, network security groups, and virtual private networks (VPNs) to control traffic flow and restrict access to resources. Segmentation of networks using virtual LANs (VLANs) or virtual private clouds (VPCs) enhances network security.

Vulnerability scanning and patch management are crucial practices for IaaS security. Organizations should regularly scan their cloud resources for vulnerabilities and apply security patches and updates promptly. Vulnerability management tools can help automate this process.

Implementing security policies and compliance standards is essential for maintaining a secure IaaS environment. Organizations should define security policies that align with industry standards and regulations. Compliance checks should be performed regularly to ensure that resources meet security requirements.

Regularly backing up data and creating disaster recovery plans are essential practices for data protection in IaaS environments. Organizations should schedule automated backups of critical data and applications and test their disaster recovery procedures to ensure business continuity in the event of disruptions.

Container security is a consideration for organizations using container orchestration platforms, such as Kubernetes, in IaaS environments. Implementing container security best practices, such as scanning container images for vulnerabilities and applying security policies, helps protect containerized applications.

Managing secrets and sensitive information securely is critical in IaaS environments. Organizations should use secrets management services to store and access sensitive information, such as API keys and passwords, securely. Secrets should be rotated regularly to reduce the risk of exposure.

Implementing network segmentation and access controls is essential for IaaS performance optimization. By segmenting networks and controlling access to resources, organizations can reduce network congestion and improve overall network performance.

Resource monitoring and performance tuning are ongoing activities for IaaS performance optimization. Organizations should use monitoring tools to track resource utilization and performance metrics. Performance tuning involves adjusting resource configurations, such as CPU, memory, and storage, to optimize application performance.

Implementing load balancing and content delivery networks (CDNs) can significantly improve application performance. Load balancers distribute incoming traffic across multiple instances, improving application availability and responsiveness. CDNs cache content closer to end-users, reducing latency and improving content delivery.

Using auto-scaling and resource scaling strategies is essential for managing performance in dynamic workloads. Auto-scaling allows resources to automatically adjust to changing workloads, ensuring that applications have sufficient capacity during peak demand.

Optimizing storage performance involves selecting the appropriate storage type and configuration for data storage needs. Organizations should consider factors such as input/output operations per second (IOPS), latency, and throughput when choosing storage options. Utilizing storage tiering and caching mechanisms can further enhance storage performance.

Database performance optimization is critical for applications that rely on databases. Organizations should regularly review and optimize database queries, indexing, and caching strategies. Implementing managed database services can offload administrative tasks and improve database performance.

Resource rightsizing is an essential practice for IaaS cost optimization and performance. Organizations should periodically review resource sizes and configurations to ensure they match workload requirements. Oversized or underutilized resources should be resized to optimize costs and performance.

Leveraging cloud cost management tools and platforms can help organizations monitor and optimize resource costs and performance. These tools provide insights into cost breakdowns, spending trends, and performance bottlenecks. Organizations can use these insights to make data-driven decisions.

Resource governance and policy enforcement are essential for maintaining performance and security in IaaS environments. Organizations should define and enforce resource naming conventions, access controls, and compliance policies. Governance controls help maintain resource consistency and security.

In summary, IaaS best practices for security and performance are essential for organizations seeking to maximize the benefits of cloud computing while ensuring the confidentiality, integrity, and availability of their data and applications. By implementing robust security measures, monitoring and optimizing resource performance, and adhering to best practices, organizations can achieve a secure and high-performing IaaS environment.

The landscape of Infrastructure as a Service (IaaS) is continually evolving, driven by technological advancements, changing business needs, and the pursuit of greater efficiency and innovation. As organizations increasingly rely on IaaS to power their digital transformation journeys, several emerging trends are shaping the future of IaaS and influencing how businesses leverage cloud infrastructure.

One of the prominent trends in the world of IaaS is the growing adoption of serverless computing. Serverless computing abstracts away the underlying infrastructure management, allowing developers to focus solely on writing code and deploying applications. This paradigm shift is reshaping the way applications are developed and operated in the cloud, enabling more rapid development and reduced operational overhead.

The proliferation of edge computing is another trend that is gaining traction in the IaaS space. Edge computing involves processing data closer to the source of data generation, which reduces latency and enhances real-time decision-making. Organizations are increasingly deploying edge infrastructure to support applications requiring low-latency responses, such as IoT devices and autonomous vehicles.

Hybrid and multi-cloud strategies continue to be at the forefront of IaaS trends. Many organizations are adopting a hybrid approach that combines on-premises infrastructure with public and private cloud resources. This allows them to maintain control over sensitive data and applications while leveraging the scalability and flexibility of the cloud. Multi-cloud strategies, which involve using multiple cloud providers, are also on the rise to avoid vendor lock-in and enhance redundancy.

Artificial Intelligence (AI) and Machine Learning (ML) are becoming integral components of IaaS solutions. Cloud providers are offering AI and ML services that enable organizations to harness the power of these technologies without the need for extensive expertise. These services empower businesses to build AI-driven applications, analyze data, and gain insights at scale.

Containerization and Kubernetes orchestration are transforming the way applications are packaged, deployed, and managed in IaaS environments. Containers provide a lightweight and consistent runtime environment, making it easier to develop and deploy applications across different cloud platforms. Kubernetes, an open-source container orchestration platform, simplifies container management, scaling, and orchestration.

The adoption of DevOps practices in conjunction with IaaS is accelerating the delivery of software and services. DevOps fosters collaboration between development and operations teams, enabling continuous integration, continuous delivery (CI/CD), and automated deployment. This approach enhances agility and reduces time-to-market for applications and updates.

Edge AI, which combines edge computing and AI capabilities, is an emerging trend poised to revolutionize various industries. Edge AI brings machine learning models to the edge devices, enabling real-time processing of data and decision-making. This trend has applications in fields like autonomous vehicles, robotics, and industrial automation.

Quantum computing is on the horizon as a game-changing technology with potential implications for IaaS. While quantum computing is still in its early stages, cloud providers are exploring ways to make quantum computing resources available to organizations for research and development purposes. Quantum computing has the potential to address complex problems that are currently beyond the reach of classical computing.

Serverless containers are an evolving trend that combines the benefits of serverless computing with container technology. This approach allows developers to run containerized workloads without managing the underlying container infrastructure. Serverless containers provide the scalability and cost-effectiveness of serverless computing while accommodating containerized applications.

Zero Trust security models are gaining prominence in IaaS environments as organizations seek to enhance their security posture. Zero Trust assumes that threats can originate from within and outside the network, requiring continuous verification of users and devices. This approach ensures that access to resources is only granted to authenticated and authorized entities.

Energy efficiency and sustainability are increasingly important considerations in IaaS design and operation. Cloud providers are investing in renewable energy sources and data center cooling technologies to reduce their environmental impact. Organizations are also looking for ways to optimize resource usage to minimize energy consumption.

Serverless databases, also known as database as a service (DBaaS), are emerging as a trend that simplifies database management in IaaS environments. These managed database services handle tasks such as provisioning, scaling, and backups, freeing organizations from database administration tasks and reducing operational overhead.

Blockchain technology is being integrated into IaaS solutions to enhance security and transparency in various industries. Blockchain can be used for secure data sharing, supply chain management, and digital identity verification. Cloud providers are offering blockchain-as-a-service (BaaS) platforms to simplify blockchain development and deployment.

Edge-native applications are becoming more prevalent with the rise of edge computing. These applications are designed to run efficiently at the edge of the network, where resources may be limited. Edge-native development frameworks and tools are emerging to support the creation of applications tailored to edge environments.

In summary, the future of IaaS is marked by a dynamic landscape driven by technological innovations and evolving business requirements. Trends such as serverless computing, edge computing, AI/ML integration, and hybrid/multi-cloud strategies are reshaping how organizations leverage cloud infrastructure. As organizations navigate this evolving landscape, staying informed about these trends and their potential impacts is essential for making informed decisions and driving digital transformation in the IaaS era.

Book 2
Mastering IaaS
Building Scalable Cloud Solutions with AWS and GCE

ROB BOTWRIGHT

Chapter 1: The Evolution of Cloud Infrastructure

The historical origins of cloud computing can be traced back to the early days of computing and the development of networked systems. While the term "cloud computing" itself is relatively recent, the concepts and technologies that underpin it have evolved over several decades.

In the 1960s, the concept of time-sharing emerged, allowing multiple users to access a single computer system simultaneously. This laid the foundation for the idea of resource sharing and remote access to computing power.

During the 1970s, the development of packet-switched networks, such as ARPANET, the precursor to the internet, enabled distributed computing and remote access to computing resources. This era saw the birth of the client-server model, where users accessed resources from centralized servers.

The 1980s witnessed the proliferation of personal computers (PCs) and the growth of client-server computing. Organizations deployed server-based systems to manage data and applications, and PCs became the primary interface for users to access these resources.

In the 1990s, the internet became more accessible to the public, leading to the rise of the World Wide Web. This era marked the beginning of the shift toward web-based applications and services, with companies like Amazon and eBay pioneering online commerce.

The term "cloud computing" started to gain traction in the early 2000s, although its precise definition and scope were still evolving. In 2006, Amazon Web Services (AWS) launched Amazon Elastic Compute Cloud (Amazon EC2), one of the first widely adopted cloud computing platforms, providing scalable virtualized computing resources.

Around the same time, Google introduced Google Apps, a suite of web-based productivity tools, and services. These developments signaled the emergence of cloud-based software as a service (SaaS) offerings, challenging traditional software distribution models.

In 2008, the U.S. National Institute of Standards and Technology (NIST) published its definition of cloud computing, establishing a standardized framework that included essential characteristics, service models, and deployment models. This NIST definition helped clarify the concept of cloud computing and provided a basis for its widespread adoption.

The following years saw the rapid expansion of cloud computing services, with providers like Microsoft Azure and Google Cloud Platform (GCP) entering the market. Cloud computing began to offer a wide range of services, from infrastructure as a service (IaaS) and platform as a service (PaaS) to specialized services like machine learning and big data analytics.

The adoption of cloud computing gained momentum across various industries, driven by the benefits of scalability, cost-effectiveness, and flexibility. Enterprises started migrating their IT infrastructure and applications to the cloud, leading to the transformation of IT operations.

Cloud providers continued to innovate and expand their global data center networks, ensuring high availability and reliability for customers. The advent of serverless computing, container orchestration with Kubernetes, and edge computing further expanded the possibilities of cloud-based solutions.

As cloud computing evolved, the industry saw the development of hybrid cloud and multi-cloud strategies, enabling organizations to combine on-premises infrastructure with public and private cloud resources. These approaches offered greater flexibility and allowed businesses to address specific compliance and data residency requirements.

Security and compliance became central concerns in the cloud computing landscape. Cloud providers invested heavily in security measures and compliance certifications to address customer concerns and regulatory requirements. Encryption, identity and access management, and threat detection became critical components of cloud security.

The rise of artificial intelligence (AI) and machine learning (ML) also had a significant impact on cloud computing. Cloud providers offered AI/ML services that enabled organizations to harness the power of these technologies without the need for extensive expertise. These services fueled innovation in areas like natural language processing, computer vision, and predictive analytics.

In recent years, the cloud computing industry has continued to evolve, with a focus on sustainability and environmental responsibility. Cloud providers have committed to using renewable energy sources and implementing energy-efficient data center designs to reduce their carbon footprint.

The COVID-19 pandemic further accelerated the adoption of cloud technologies, as remote work and digital transformation became imperative for businesses worldwide. Cloud-based collaboration tools, remote access solutions, and scalable infrastructure played a crucial role in supporting the remote workforce.

Looking ahead, the future of cloud computing is expected to be shaped by emerging technologies such as quantum computing, 5G networks, and edge computing. These technologies have the potential to unlock new possibilities in areas like real-time data processing, advanced analytics, and immersive experiences.

In summary, the historical origins of cloud computing can be traced back to the evolution of computing, networking, and the internet. The concept of cloud computing has come a long way, transforming the way organizations access and manage IT resources. As cloud computing continues to evolve, it will remain a driving force behind innovation and digital transformation in the modern era.

The development of cloud infrastructure has been marked by several significant milestones that have shaped the evolution of cloud computing and its impact on businesses and technology.

One of the earliest milestones in cloud infrastructure development was the concept of time-sharing, which emerged in the 1960s. Time-sharing allowed multiple users to access a single computer system simultaneously, laying the foundation for the idea of resource sharing and remote access to computing power.

In the 1970s, the advent of packet-switched networks, including ARPANET, paved the way for distributed computing and remote access to resources. This era saw the emergence of the client-server model, where users accessed resources from centralized servers, a concept that would later become fundamental in cloud computing.

The 1980s marked the proliferation of personal computers (PCs) and the growth of client-server computing. Organizations began to deploy server-based systems to manage data and applications, with PCs serving as the primary interface for users to access these resources.

In the 1990s, the internet became more accessible to the public, leading to the rise of the World Wide Web. This transformative period marked the beginning of the shift toward web-based applications and services, with companies like Amazon and eBay pioneering online commerce.

The term "cloud computing" started to gain recognition in the early 2000s, although its precise definition and scope were still evolving. In 2006, Amazon Web Services (AWS) launched Amazon Elastic Compute Cloud (Amazon EC2), one of the first widely adopted cloud computing platforms, providing scalable virtualized computing resources.

Around the same time, Google introduced Google Apps, a suite of web-based productivity tools and services. These developments signaled the emergence of cloud-based software as a service (SaaS) offerings, challenging traditional software distribution models.

In 2008, the U.S. National Institute of Standards and Technology (NIST) published its official definition of cloud computing, providing a standardized framework that included essential characteristics, service models, and deployment models. This NIST definition played a pivotal role in clarifying the concept of cloud computing and provided a foundation for its widespread adoption.

The following years witnessed the rapid expansion of cloud computing services, with providers like Microsoft Azure and Google Cloud Platform (GCP) entering the market. Cloud computing began to offer a wide range of services, from infrastructure as a service (IaaS) and platform as a service (PaaS) to specialized services like machine learning and big data analytics.

The adoption of cloud computing gained momentum across various industries, driven by the benefits of scalability, cost-effectiveness, and flexibility. Enterprises started migrating their IT infrastructure and applications to the cloud, leading to a transformation of IT operations.

Cloud providers continued to innovate and expand their global data center networks, ensuring high availability and reliability for customers. The advent of serverless computing, container orchestration with Kubernetes, and edge computing further expanded the possibilities of cloud-based solutions.

As cloud computing evolved, the industry saw the development of hybrid cloud and multi-cloud strategies, enabling organizations to combine on-premises infrastructure with public and private cloud resources. These approaches offered greater flexibility and allowed businesses to address specific compliance and data residency requirements.

Security and compliance became central concerns in the cloud computing landscape. Cloud providers invested heavily in security measures and compliance certifications to address customer concerns and regulatory requirements. Encryption, identity and access management, and threat detection became critical components of cloud security.

The rise of artificial intelligence (AI) and machine learning (ML) also had a significant impact on cloud computing. Cloud providers offered AI and ML services that enabled organizations to harness the power of these technologies without the need for extensive expertise. These services empowered businesses to build AI-driven applications, analyze data, and gain insights at scale.

In recent years, the cloud computing industry has continued to evolve, with a focus on sustainability and environmental responsibility. Cloud providers have committed to using renewable energy sources and implementing energy-efficient data center designs to reduce their carbon footprint.

The COVID-19 pandemic further accelerated the adoption of cloud technologies, as remote work and digital transformation became imperative for businesses worldwide. Cloud-based collaboration tools, remote access solutions, and scalable infrastructure played a crucial role in supporting the remote workforce.

Looking ahead, the future of cloud computing is expected to be shaped by emerging technologies such as quantum computing, 5G networks, and edge computing. These technologies have the potential to unlock new possibilities in areas like real-time data processing, advanced analytics, and immersive experiences.

In summary, the development of cloud infrastructure has been marked by significant milestones, from the early days of time-sharing and client-server computing to the emergence of cloud computing as a transformative force in modern IT. These milestones have shaped the evolution of cloud computing and continue to drive innovation and digital transformation across industries.

Chapter 2: Deep Dive into AWS: Amazon Web Services

Amazon Web Services (AWS) offers a vast and diverse array of cloud services and solutions designed to meet the needs of organizations of all sizes and industries.

Compute Services:

AWS provides a wide range of compute services, including Amazon Elastic Compute Cloud (EC2), which offers resizable virtual machines (instances) for running applications, and AWS Lambda, a serverless computing service that enables you to run code in response to events without managing servers.

Storage Services:

AWS offers various storage services, such as Amazon Simple Storage Service (S3), a scalable object storage service, and Amazon Elastic Block Store (EBS), which provides block storage volumes for use with EC2 instances. Additionally, Amazon Glacier offers long-term data archival and backup.

Networking Services:

AWS includes networking services like Amazon Virtual Private Cloud (VPC), which enables you to create isolated network environments, and Amazon Route 53, a scalable domain name system (DNS) web service. AWS Direct Connect allows for dedicated network connections to the AWS cloud.

Database Services:

Database services in AWS comprise Amazon Relational Database Service (RDS) for managed relational databases, Amazon DynamoDB for NoSQL databases, and Amazon Aurora for high-performance, fully managed databases.

Analytics Services:

AWS offers a suite of analytics services, including Amazon Redshift for data warehousing, Amazon EMR for big data processing, and Amazon QuickSight for business intelligence and data visualization.

Security and Identity Services:

AWS provides robust security and identity services such as AWS Identity and Access Management (IAM) for access control, AWS Key Management Service (KMS) for encryption key management, and AWS Security Hub for centralized security management.

Machine Learning Services:

AWS offers machine learning services like Amazon SageMaker for building, training, and deploying machine learning models, as well as services like Amazon Rekognition for image and video analysis and Amazon Comprehend for natural language processing.

Application Integration Services:

AWS includes services such as Amazon Simple Queue Service (SQS) for message queuing, Amazon Simple Notification Service (SNS) for event-driven messaging, and AWS Step Functions for building serverless workflows.

Developer Tools:

Developer tools in AWS encompass services like AWS CodeDeploy for automating code deployments, AWS CodeBuild for building and testing code, and AWS CodePipeline for continuous integration and continuous delivery (CI/CD).

Management and Governance Services:

AWS provides management and governance services, including AWS CloudFormation for infrastructure as code, AWS Config for resource inventory and compliance, and AWS Organizations for managing multiple AWS accounts.

IoT (Internet of Things) Services:

AWS IoT services enable the connection and management of IoT devices and data, including AWS IoT Core for device messaging, AWS IoT Greengrass for edge computing, and AWS IoT Analytics for IoT data analysis.

Migration and Transfer Services:

AWS offers services like AWS DataSync for data transfer and migration, AWS Server Migration Service (SMS) for migrating on-premises workloads, and AWS Snowball for large-scale data transfers.

Application Services:

Application services include AWS App Runner for building and running containerized applications, AWS App Mesh for microservices communication, and Amazon Simple Email Service (SES) for sending emails.

Customer Engagement Services:

AWS provides customer engagement services like Amazon Connect for cloud-based contact centers, Amazon Pinpoint for targeted customer engagement, and Amazon Polly for text-to-speech conversion.

Blockchain Services:

AWS offers blockchain services, including Amazon Managed Blockchain for building and managing blockchain networks, and Amazon Quantum Ledger Database (QLDB) for ledger databases with transparent and immutable history.

Quantum Technologies:

Quantum computing services are emerging, with Amazon Braket allowing customers to experiment with quantum algorithms and hardware from leading quantum computing providers.

End-User Computing:

End-user computing services in AWS include Amazon WorkSpaces for virtual desktops, Amazon AppStream 2.0 for application streaming, and Amazon WorkLink for secure mobile access to internal web content.

Satellite and Ground Station:

AWS Ground Station provides satellite communication capabilities, allowing customers to control and process satellite data in the cloud.

In summary, AWS offers a comprehensive suite of cloud services across various categories, empowering organizations to build, deploy, and manage a wide range of applications and solutions in the cloud. These services cover computing, storage, networking, databases, analytics, security, machine learning, and more, enabling businesses to innovate and scale with flexibility and efficiency in the AWS cloud environment.

The AWS Management Console and Command Line Interface (CLI) are two essential tools for interacting with and managing your AWS resources and services in the cloud.

The AWS Management Console is a web-based user interface that provides a graphical way to access and manage your AWS resources.

It offers a user-friendly experience, allowing you to navigate through different services, view resource details, and perform various tasks with just a few clicks.

The Console is accessible from any web browser and provides a visual representation of your AWS infrastructure, making it easy to monitor and control your resources.

While the AWS Management Console is a powerful and intuitive tool, it may not be the most efficient option for automating repetitive tasks or managing resources at scale.

That's where the AWS Command Line Interface (CLI) comes into play.

The AWS CLI is a command-line tool that allows you to interact with AWS services through text-based commands.

It provides a command-line interface for AWS, enabling you to perform actions, configure resources, and automate tasks programmatically.

The AWS CLI is available for Windows, macOS, and Linux, making it accessible from various operating systems.

One of the key advantages of using the AWS CLI is its scripting and automation capabilities.

You can write scripts and use the CLI to create, update, and manage AWS resources in a programmatic and repeatable way.

This is particularly useful for tasks such as provisioning infrastructure, configuring security settings, and deploying applications.

To get started with the AWS CLI, you need to install it on your local machine and configure it with your AWS credentials.

Once configured, you can use the CLI to interact with AWS services by running commands that correspond to specific AWS actions.

For example, you can create an EC2 instance, list S3 buckets, or configure IAM roles using the CLI.

The AWS CLI uses a simple syntax that consists of commands, subcommands, and options.

Commands represent the AWS service you want to interact with, subcommands specify the specific action, and options provide additional parameters and settings.

For example, the command "aws ec2 describe-instances" retrieves information about EC2 instances in your AWS account.

Here, "aws" is the main command, "ec2" is the service, and "describe-instances" is the action.

The AWS CLI also supports output formatting, allowing you to choose the output format for the information returned by AWS services.

Common output formats include JSON, text, and table, making it easier to parse and process the data.

While the AWS CLI provides a powerful and flexible way to manage AWS resources, it does require familiarity with command-line interfaces and scripting.

If you prefer a graphical interface or need to perform occasional tasks without scripting, the AWS Management Console is a convenient choice.

The AWS Management Console and AWS CLI are not mutually exclusive; you can use them together based on your specific needs and preferences.

For example, you might use the Console for initial resource configuration and management and then switch to the CLI for automated and scripted tasks.

In addition to the AWS CLI, AWS provides SDKs (Software Development Kits) for various programming languages.

SDKs enable developers to interact with AWS services in their preferred programming language, making it easier to integrate AWS functionality into applications.

The AWS Management Console and CLI are part of a broader ecosystem of AWS tools and services designed to simplify and streamline cloud management.

These tools cater to different user preferences and requirements, allowing you to choose the best approach for your specific use cases.

In summary, the AWS Management Console and AWS CLI are essential tools for managing AWS resources and services.

The Console offers a graphical interface for easy resource management, while the CLI provides a programmatic and scriptable way to interact with AWS.

Both tools are valuable additions to your AWS toolkit, and their combined use can help you efficiently manage your cloud infrastructure and applications.

Chapter 3: GCE in Depth: Google Cloud Engine

Google Cloud Compute Engine, often referred to as GCE, is a fundamental component of the Google Cloud Platform (GCP) that provides highly scalable and flexible virtual machine (VM) instances for a wide range of computing workloads.

One of the prominent features of Google Cloud Compute Engine is its ability to offer a vast selection of pre-configured virtual machine instances known as "machine types," catering to different performance, memory, and CPU requirements.

These machine types include standard, high-memory, high-CPU, and custom machine types, allowing users to choose the configuration that best suits their application's needs.

Google Cloud Compute Engine is designed to deliver consistent and reliable performance by leveraging Google's global network infrastructure, ensuring low-latency network connectivity and high availability.

Users can select from various operating systems and images, including popular Linux distributions and Windows Server, making it easy to run their preferred software stacks on GCE instances.

One notable feature of Compute Engine is the option to create custom images, enabling users to create customized VM instances with specific configurations and software installations.

Google Cloud Compute Engine offers robust networking capabilities, including Virtual Private Cloud (VPC) for network segmentation and isolation, as well as advanced networking features like load balancing and Cloud DNS for efficient traffic distribution and domain management.

To enhance security, Compute Engine provides features such as firewalls, Identity and Access Management (IAM) controls, and private communication within VPCs, ensuring that users can build secure and isolated environments for their applications.

Another powerful feature of Compute Engine is the ability to attach and manage persistent disks, which can be used to store data and configurations independently of VM instances, allowing for data persistence even if an instance is deleted.

Compute Engine instances can be configured to automatically scale vertically (resizing) and horizontally (load balancing) based on application demands, providing a high degree of flexibility and agility.

Users can take advantage of Google Cloud's global presence to deploy Compute Engine instances in multiple regions and availability zones, enhancing fault tolerance and disaster recovery capabilities.

Compute Engine offers multiple options for data storage, including Google Cloud Storage, Cloud SQL for managed relational databases, and Cloud Spanner for globally distributed databases, enabling users to select the right storage solution for their applications.

Google Cloud's emphasis on sustainability is reflected in Compute Engine's commitment to green energy and carbon neutrality, aligning with environmentally conscious practices.

To simplify management and automation, Compute Engine provides integration with Google Kubernetes Engine (GKE) for container orchestration and Google Cloud Deployment Manager for infrastructure as code (IAC) deployments.

Users can also benefit from Compute Engine's integration with other Google Cloud services, such as Google Cloud Monitoring and Logging, for enhanced observability and troubleshooting capabilities.

Compute Engine offers various pricing options, including on-demand, preemptible (short-lived and cost-effective), and custom pricing plans, allowing users to optimize their cloud spending based on workload requirements.

With the introduction of Confidential VMs, Google Cloud Compute Engine offers a unique security feature that allows users to run workloads in an environment protected by Google's Confidential Computing technology, safeguarding sensitive data and code from potential threats.

Additionally, Compute Engine provides support for GPU instances, enabling users to leverage graphical processing units for tasks like machine learning, scientific simulations, and high-performance computing.

Google Cloud Compute Engine's commitment to customer support includes multiple support tiers, ensuring that users have access to the level of assistance and expertise they require for their cloud projects.

Compute Engine instances can be managed and monitored using the Google Cloud Console, the Cloud SDK command-line tool, and APIs, providing a seamless experience for developers and administrators.

In summary, Google Cloud Compute Engine offers a robust and flexible platform for running virtual machine instances in the cloud. Its feature-rich environment includes a wide range of machine types, extensive networking capabilities, security features, and integration with other Google Cloud services. Compute Engine is designed to meet the demands of modern applications and workloads, providing users with the tools they need to build and scale their cloud infrastructure effectively.

Managing Google Cloud Compute Engine (GCE) instances and disks is a critical aspect of effectively utilizing the resources provided by the Google Cloud Platform (GCP).

GCE instances are virtual machines (VMs) that run within the GCP infrastructure, and they can be easily created, configured, and managed to support various workloads and applications.

One of the primary tasks in managing GCE instances is the creation process, which involves selecting the desired machine type, choosing an operating system image, configuring networking settings, and specifying disk storage options.

Once created, GCE instances can be accessed and controlled through the Google Cloud Console, the Google Cloud SDK command-line tool, or programmatically using GCP APIs, offering multiple avenues for management.

GCE instances can be customized with various operating system distributions and software stacks, allowing users to tailor their VMs to specific application requirements.

Disk management is a crucial aspect of GCE instance management, as disks store data and configurations independently of VM instances.

GCE instances typically have at least one boot disk that contains the operating system and application software, and additional data disks can be attached to provide additional storage capacity.

Google Cloud offers different types of disks, including standard persistent disks, SSD persistent disks for high-performance I/O, and local SSDs that provide temporary and high-speed storage.

One essential aspect of managing GCE instances and disks is ensuring data persistence and durability, which can be achieved by taking advantage of Google Cloud Storage and snapshotting features.

Snapshots allow users to capture point-in-time copies of disks, providing a backup mechanism that can be used for disaster recovery or replicating data across regions.

Another critical aspect of GCE instance management is network configuration, where Google Cloud Virtual Private

Cloud (VPC) plays a central role in providing network isolation and segmentation.

Users can create custom VPC networks with subnets, control firewall rules, and manage routes to ensure secure communication between GCE instances and other cloud resources.

Google Cloud provides a variety of networking features, such as load balancing, Cloud DNS, and Cloud Interconnect, to enhance the connectivity and reliability of GCE instances.

Scaling GCE instances horizontally and vertically is a fundamental part of managing workloads efficiently, as it allows resources to be adjusted dynamically based on application demand.

Vertical scaling involves resizing GCE instances to meet increased or decreased resource requirements, while horizontal scaling involves load balancing across multiple instances to distribute traffic evenly.

To automate and streamline the management of GCE instances and infrastructure, Google Cloud offers tools like Google Cloud Deployment Manager, which allows users to define their infrastructure as code (IAC) using templates.

Infrastructure as code (IAC) enables users to declare the desired state of their cloud resources using code, making it easier to replicate and manage infrastructure configurations consistently.

Users can also take advantage of Google Kubernetes Engine (GKE) to orchestrate and manage containerized applications at scale, with GCE instances serving as worker nodes in Kubernetes clusters.

Monitoring and maintaining GCE instances are ongoing tasks that involve tracking resource utilization, monitoring system health, and applying security updates and patches.

Google Cloud offers monitoring and logging services, such as Google Cloud Monitoring and Google Cloud Logging, to help users gain insights into the performance and behavior of their GCE instances.

Security plays a crucial role in managing GCE instances, and Google Cloud provides features like Identity and Access Management (IAM), firewall rules, and Virtual Private Cloud (VPC) security controls to ensure that resources are protected against unauthorized access and threats.

Users can also take advantage of Google Cloud Security Command Center to gain visibility into security threats and vulnerabilities within their GCP environment.

To streamline repetitive tasks and automate management workflows, users can leverage the Google Cloud SDK and Google Cloud APIs, allowing programmatic interaction with GCE instances and resources.

Google Cloud offers a range of support and assistance options, including different support tiers, documentation, and a community of users and experts, to provide help and guidance in managing GCE instances effectively.

In summary, managing Google Cloud Compute Engine (GCE) instances and disks is a fundamental aspect of cloud infrastructure management within the Google Cloud Platform (GCP).

Effective management involves creating and configuring GCE instances, attaching and managing disks, configuring networking and security settings, and ensuring data persistence and durability through snapshots and backups.

Monitoring, scaling, and automation are essential components of GCE instance management, and Google Cloud provides a suite of tools and services to facilitate these tasks.

By mastering the management of GCE instances and resources, users can optimize their cloud infrastructure to support a wide range of workloads and applications efficiently.

Chapter 4: Networking and Connectivity in the Cloud

Cloud networking is a foundational element of modern cloud computing, serving as the backbone that connects and facilitates communication between various cloud resources and services.

It plays a critical role in enabling organizations to harness the power of the cloud by providing the necessary infrastructure to securely transmit data and deliver applications and services to users.

At its core, cloud networking is about establishing and managing the connections and data pathways that enable the flow of information within a cloud environment and between on-premises and cloud resources.

One of the fundamental concepts in cloud networking is the virtual network, which is a software-defined representation of a traditional physical network.

Virtual networks provide isolation and segmentation, allowing organizations to create private, secure communication channels within the cloud to safeguard data and resources.

These virtual networks can be customized to align with specific requirements, ensuring that traffic flows as intended while meeting security and compliance needs.

In cloud networking, the concept of a Virtual Private Cloud (VPC) is common, and it serves as the foundation for network segmentation and isolation within cloud environments.

A VPC allows organizations to create multiple isolated networks, each with its own set of rules and security configurations, ensuring that resources within one VPC cannot communicate with resources in another without explicit permission.

Cloud networking also incorporates the concept of subnets, which are subdivisions of a VPC that further enable network segmentation.

Subnets can be associated with specific availability zones or regions, providing flexibility in designing network architectures that support high availability and fault tolerance.

One of the key advantages of cloud networking is the ability to scale and adapt networks to meet evolving demands.

With traditional on-premises networking, adding or modifying network infrastructure could be a time-consuming and complex process, often involving physical hardware changes.

In contrast, cloud networking allows for dynamic scaling and configuration changes through software-defined networking (SDN), reducing the time and effort required to adapt to changing requirements.

Dynamic scaling is especially valuable when considering the elasticity of cloud resources, as organizations can automatically adjust network capacity to match changes in workload demand.

Cloud providers offer various tools and services to manage and optimize cloud networking, including load balancers that distribute traffic across multiple instances or resources to ensure high availability and improve application performance.

Content delivery networks (CDNs) are another essential component of cloud networking, designed to accelerate content delivery and reduce latency by caching and distributing content closer to end-users.

Security is a paramount concern in cloud networking, and cloud providers offer a range of features and services to protect network resources and data.

Firewalls, network security groups, and access control lists (ACLs) are used to define rules and policies that control traffic flow and restrict unauthorized access to resources.

Identity and access management (IAM) is integrated into cloud networking to manage user access and permissions for network resources, ensuring that only authorized individuals or entities can make changes or access sensitive information.

Encryption is a crucial aspect of cloud networking security, and it is used to protect data in transit and at rest.

Secure Sockets Layer (SSL) and Transport Layer Security (TLS) are commonly used to encrypt data in transit, while data encryption solutions like AWS Key Management Service (KMS) and Google Cloud Key Management Service (KMS) are employed to encrypt data at rest.

Multi-factor authentication (MFA) is another security layer that helps ensure that only authorized individuals can access and manage network resources.

One of the significant advantages of cloud networking is its ability to support hybrid and multi-cloud environments, where organizations can seamlessly integrate on-premises data centers with cloud resources and services.

This flexibility allows businesses to transition to the cloud at their own pace, enabling hybrid scenarios that combine the strengths of both on-premises and cloud infrastructures.

Networking technologies like Virtual Private Network (VPN) and Direct Connect provide secure connections between on-premises and cloud environments, ensuring seamless communication and data transfer.

As organizations continue to adopt cloud networking, the industry has witnessed the emergence of Software-Defined Wide Area Network (SD-WAN) solutions.

SD-WAN technology optimizes network performance by intelligently routing traffic across multiple network paths, including private and public connections, to ensure the best possible user experience.

In summary, cloud networking is a foundational element of modern cloud computing, enabling organizations to connect, scale, and secure their cloud resources and services.

Key concepts such as virtual networks, Virtual Private Clouds (VPCs), subnets, and software-defined networking (SDN) empower organizations to design and manage network architectures that meet their specific needs.

Security features, dynamic scaling, and support for hybrid and multi-cloud environments further enhance the capabilities of cloud networking, making it a critical component for organizations looking to leverage the full potential of the cloud.

Virtual Private Clouds (VPCs) serve as the foundation for network isolation and segmentation within cloud environments, providing organizations with the means to create private and secure communication channels.

VPCs enable organizations to define and control their cloud network's architecture, allowing for customization to meet specific security, performance, and compliance requirements.

When designing a VPC, one of the first considerations is defining the address space, which involves specifying the range of IP addresses that will be used for resources within the VPC.

Address space planning is essential to avoid IP address conflicts and ensure efficient resource allocation.

VPCs are typically associated with a specific region and availability zone within a cloud provider's infrastructure, allowing organizations to deploy resources in a way that enhances availability and fault tolerance.

Subnets are subdivisions of VPCs, and they further enable network segmentation and isolation by dividing the VPC's IP address range into smaller, manageable blocks.

Subnets can be associated with specific availability zones or regions, providing flexibility in designing network architectures that support high availability and redundancy.

Each subnet is associated with a route table, which determines how traffic is routed within the subnet and to external destinations.

Route tables can be customized to control traffic flow, making it possible to implement security policies and control access between subnets.

VPCs also support network access control lists (ACLs) and security groups, which are used to define rules and policies for controlling inbound and outbound traffic.

Network ACLs are stateless and operate at the subnet level, while security groups are stateful and operate at the instance level, allowing for fine-grained control over traffic.

A well-designed VPC architecture considers factors such as security, availability, and performance.

For security, it is common to create separate subnets for different security zones, isolating resources with different security requirements.

For example, public-facing resources like web servers might be placed in a public subnet, while databases and internal services are located in private subnets.

To enhance availability, organizations can distribute resources across multiple availability zones to ensure that if one zone experiences an outage, resources in other zones remain accessible.

This redundancy minimizes downtime and improves fault tolerance.

Performance considerations involve optimizing network traffic by choosing the appropriate instance types and configurations for the intended workload.

Additionally, organizations can utilize content delivery networks (CDNs) and load balancers to optimize traffic distribution and reduce latency.

When designing VPCs, it is crucial to plan for future growth and scalability.

A VPC's address space should accommodate potential resource expansion without the need for major address reconfiguration.

This foresight ensures that as an organization's cloud footprint grows, the VPC can scale with minimal disruptions.

To maintain security and compliance, organizations should regularly review and update network ACLs, security groups, and routing rules to align with evolving requirements and best practices.

Monitoring and logging tools provided by cloud providers can help organizations gain insights into network traffic, allowing them to detect and respond to potential security threats and performance issues.

Advanced features like Virtual Private Network (VPN) connections and Direct Connect enable secure and high-performance connectivity between on-premises data centers and cloud resources within a VPC.

These features facilitate hybrid and multi-cloud architectures, allowing organizations to leverage cloud resources while maintaining connectivity with their existing infrastructure.

In summary, Virtual Private Clouds (VPCs) and subnet design are foundational elements of cloud networking, providing organizations with the means to create secure and customized network architectures.

Address space planning, security controls, availability considerations, and performance optimization are key factors in designing effective VPCs.

Regular monitoring and updates ensure that VPCs remain aligned with evolving requirements and industry best practices, enabling organizations to build and maintain robust and scalable cloud networks.

Chapter 5: Data Storage Solutions for Scalability

Cloud storage services offer a wide range of options for storing, managing, and accessing data in the cloud.

These services have become essential components of modern computing, enabling individuals and organizations to securely store and retrieve their data from anywhere with an internet connection.

There are several types of cloud storage services available, each designed to meet specific needs and use cases.

One of the most common types of cloud storage services is file storage, which allows users to upload and store individual files and documents in the cloud.

File storage services are often used for personal data backup, file sharing, and collaboration, providing a convenient way to access files from multiple devices.

Well-known file storage services include Dropbox, Google Drive, and Microsoft OneDrive.

Another type of cloud storage is object storage, which is designed for storing large amounts of unstructured data, such as images, videos, backups, and log files.

Object storage services organize data into objects, each with a unique identifier, and store them in a flat namespace.

This architecture makes it easy to scale storage capacity as needed and retrieve data quickly.

Prominent object storage services include Amazon S3 (Simple Storage Service), Google Cloud Storage, and Azure Blob Storage.

Block storage is a type of cloud storage that provides raw storage volumes to virtual machines and other cloud resources.

Block storage is ideal for applications that require low-level access to storage, such as databases and file systems.

Users can create, attach, and format block storage volumes as needed and mount them to cloud instances.

Well-known block storage services include Amazon EBS (Elastic Block Store), Google Persistent Disk, and Azure Managed Disks.

Cloud storage services also offer archival storage, which is optimized for long-term data retention and infrequent access.

Archival storage is cost-effective and suitable for storing data that is rarely accessed but must be retained for compliance or historical purposes.

Examples of archival storage services include Amazon Glacier, Google Cloud Storage Coldline, and Azure Archive Storage.

Cold storage is another type of cloud storage designed for infrequently accessed data, but it offers a faster retrieval time compared to archival storage.

Cold storage is suitable for data that may need to be accessed occasionally without the long retrieval times associated with archival storage.

Popular cold storage services include Amazon S3 Glacier, Google Cloud Storage Nearline, and Azure Cool Blob Storage.

Hybrid cloud storage is a combination of on-premises storage and cloud storage, allowing organizations to seamlessly integrate their existing infrastructure with cloud resources.

Hybrid cloud storage solutions provide flexibility and scalability, enabling organizations to extend their storage capacity to the cloud while maintaining control over on-premises data.

Cloud providers like AWS, Google Cloud, and Microsoft Azure offer hybrid storage solutions to facilitate integration between on-premises environments and their respective cloud platforms.

Cloud storage services also offer data backup and disaster recovery solutions, allowing organizations to protect their data from loss or damage.

These services provide automated backup and recovery capabilities, ensuring that data can be restored in the event of hardware failure, data corruption, or other disasters.

Backup and disaster recovery services are essential for business continuity and data protection.

Cloud providers offer services like AWS Backup, Google Cloud Backup, and Azure Backup to help organizations safeguard their data.

Furthermore, cloud storage services support data synchronization and data sharing, making it easy for individuals and teams to collaborate on files and documents.

Users can access and edit files from multiple devices, and changes are synchronized across all connected devices.

This capability simplifies collaboration and enhances productivity.

In addition to file sharing and synchronization, cloud storage services often offer advanced features such as versioning, which allows users to access previous versions of files and restore them if needed.

File versioning ensures data integrity and provides a safety net against accidental data loss or changes.

Encryption is a critical security feature in cloud storage services, ensuring that data remains confidential and protected from unauthorized access.

Data is encrypted both in transit and at rest, and cloud providers implement robust security measures to safeguard customer data.

Users can also implement their encryption keys for added security.

Cloud storage services offer various storage classes, each optimized for specific performance, durability, and cost characteristics.

Users can choose the storage class that best aligns with their data requirements and budget.

Storage classes include standard, frequent access, infrequent access, and archival, among others.

In summary, cloud storage services offer a diverse range of options to accommodate various data storage needs and use cases.

From file storage and object storage to block storage and archival solutions, cloud providers offer a comprehensive suite of storage services to cater to individual and organizational requirements.

These services come with a range of features, including data synchronization, backup and disaster recovery, encryption, and flexible storage classes, making it possible for users to securely store, manage, and access their data in the cloud.

Data backup and replication are fundamental components of data management and disaster recovery, providing organizations with strategies to safeguard their critical data and ensure business continuity.

Data backup involves creating copies of data and storing them in a separate location or medium to protect against data loss due to various factors, including hardware failures, data corruption, accidental deletion, and disasters.

Backup strategies are essential for ensuring that data can be restored in its entirety in case of unexpected events.

One common approach to data backup is the use of automated backup solutions, which periodically create copies of data and store them in backup repositories.

These solutions often offer features like versioning, allowing organizations to maintain historical copies of data and recover specific versions as needed.

Backup solutions can be configured to back up data at different intervals, such as hourly, daily, or weekly, depending on the organization's recovery point objectives (RPOs).

Cloud-based backup services have gained popularity due to their scalability, reliability, and ease of use.

Organizations can leverage cloud backup solutions provided by leading cloud providers like AWS, Google Cloud, and Microsoft Azure to store their data securely in the cloud.

Cloud backup services offer automated backup schedules, retention policies, and encryption to ensure data protection and availability.

Another important aspect of data backup is offsite storage, where backup copies are stored in a location physically separate from the primary data center.

This practice mitigates the risk of data loss caused by on-premises disasters such as fires, floods, or hardware failures.

Offsite storage can be achieved through a combination of on-premises backups that are periodically transferred to an offsite location or by using cloud-based backup solutions that inherently provide offsite storage.

Replication is a data protection strategy that involves creating and maintaining duplicate copies of data in real-time or near-real-time.

Replication is designed to provide high availability and reduce downtime by ensuring that a secondary copy of data is readily available if the primary copy becomes unavailable.

One of the common replication methods is synchronous replication, where data is written to the primary and secondary locations simultaneously, ensuring that both copies are always in sync.

This approach guarantees data consistency but may introduce latency in write operations due to the need for data confirmation at both locations.

Asynchronous replication, on the other hand, allows for a slight delay between data writes at the primary and secondary locations.

This approach minimizes latency but can lead to a potential data loss window, as the secondary copy may not always be up-to-date with the primary data.

Organizations should carefully consider their recovery point objectives (RPOs) when choosing between synchronous and asynchronous replication to strike a balance between data consistency and performance.

Replication can be implemented at various levels, including database-level replication, storage-level replication, and application-level replication.

Database-level replication involves replicating data between database instances, making it an effective solution for ensuring data availability in database-centric applications.

Storage-level replication replicates entire storage volumes or arrays, providing high availability at the storage layer and allowing for rapid failover in case of hardware failures.

Application-level replication replicates data at the application layer, making it suitable for scenarios where applications need to maintain their own data synchronization mechanisms.

Many cloud providers offer replication services that enable organizations to replicate data across different regions or availability zones within the cloud environment.

These services ensure data availability and resilience within the cloud infrastructure itself.

A key consideration in data backup and replication strategies is the selection of the appropriate storage media and technologies.

Traditional backup methods may use tape drives or disk-based systems for data storage, whereas modern solutions often leverage cloud storage or disk arrays.

The choice of storage media depends on factors like cost, performance, scalability, and recovery time objectives (RTOs).

Organizations must also consider data retention policies when implementing backup and replication strategies.

Data retention defines how long backup copies are retained and under what circumstances they are deleted or overwritten.

Compliance requirements and business needs play a significant role in defining data retention policies.

Regular testing of backup and replication processes is essential to ensure their effectiveness.

Testing includes performing recovery drills and validating that data can be successfully restored from backups or replicated copies.

Testing helps identify and address any issues or gaps in the data protection strategy before a real disaster occurs.

Another important aspect of data protection is data encryption, which should be implemented during backup and replication processes to secure data both at rest and in transit.

Encryption ensures that even if backup copies or replicated data are compromised, they remain unreadable without the appropriate encryption keys.

Organizations must manage encryption keys securely to prevent unauthorized access to backup and replicated data.

Ultimately, data backup and replication strategies are critical components of a comprehensive data protection and disaster recovery plan.

These strategies ensure that organizations can maintain data availability, minimize downtime, and recover data effectively in the event of unexpected events or disasters.

By selecting the right backup and replication methods, storage media, and testing procedures, organizations can establish robust data protection measures that align with their business objectives and compliance requirements.

Chapter 6: Scalable Compute Resources and Virtual Machines

Virtualization is a technology that has revolutionized the way computing resources are utilized and managed in modern data centers and cloud environments.

At its core, virtualization involves creating multiple virtual instances or representations of physical hardware on a single physical machine, allowing for the efficient sharing of resources among multiple virtual machines (VMs).

VMs are software-based representations of physical computers, complete with their own operating systems and applications.

Virtualization enables organizations to run multiple VMs on a single physical server, effectively maximizing the utilization of hardware resources.

One of the key benefits of virtualization is server consolidation, where multiple physical servers are replaced by a smaller number of more powerful servers running multiple VMs.

This consolidation leads to significant cost savings in terms of hardware, power consumption, and data center space.

Hypervisors are the software layer that makes virtualization possible by managing and controlling the VMs and their interactions with the underlying physical hardware.

There are two main types of hypervisors: Type 1 (bare-metal) and Type 2 (hosted).

Type 1 hypervisors run directly on the physical hardware, without the need for an underlying operating system.

They are highly efficient and offer superior performance because they have direct access to the hardware resources.

Prominent Type 1 hypervisors include VMware vSphere/ESXi, Microsoft Hyper-V, and KVM (Kernel-based Virtual Machine).

Type 2 hypervisors, on the other hand, run on top of an existing operating system.

They are often used for development, testing, or desktop virtualization scenarios.

Popular Type 2 hypervisors include VMware Workstation, Oracle VirtualBox, and Parallels Desktop.

Each VM operates independently, isolated from other VMs running on the same host.

This isolation ensures that a failure or issue with one VM does not impact the operation of other VMs on the same host.

VMs can run different operating systems, making it possible to consolidate a diverse set of workloads on a single physical server.

This flexibility allows organizations to run Windows, Linux, and other operating systems side by side on the same hardware.

VMs are created from templates or images, which serve as the starting point for configuring and customizing each virtual machine.

Templates are pre-configured VM images that can be quickly deployed to create new VM instances.

Organizations can create templates for different operating systems and application stacks to streamline VM provisioning.

Once a VM is created, it can be dynamically allocated resources such as CPU, memory, and storage.

Resource allocation can be adjusted on-the-fly to meet changing workload demands, ensuring efficient resource utilization.

VMs also offer the capability to take snapshots, which are point-in-time copies of a VM's state.

Snapshots are useful for creating backups, testing software changes, and reverting to previous states in case of issues.

Live migration is another valuable feature of virtualization, allowing VMs to be moved between physical hosts without downtime.

This capability is essential for load balancing, maintenance, and disaster recovery scenarios.

Virtualization technologies have evolved to include advanced features like High Availability (HA), which automatically restarts VMs on different hosts in case of host failures, and Fault Tolerance (FT), which provides continuous VM operation even in the event of hardware failures.

Security in virtualized environments is a critical consideration, and hypervisors implement various security measures to isolate VMs and protect against unauthorized access.

Hypervisor security features include secure boot, encryption, and access control mechanisms.

Containers are another form of virtualization that has gained popularity, offering a lightweight and efficient way to package and run applications and their dependencies.

Containers share the host operating system kernel, making them more lightweight and faster to start compared to traditional VMs.

Docker is a well-known containerization platform that has become the standard for deploying and managing containers.

Container orchestration tools like Kubernetes enable the automated deployment, scaling, and management of containerized applications.

Virtualization technologies have also extended to the cloud, where cloud providers offer virtualized infrastructure as a service (IaaS) platforms.

Customers can provision VMs and other resources in the cloud, taking advantage of the scalability and flexibility offered by virtualization.

In summary, virtualization and VMs have transformed the way computing resources are utilized and managed, enabling organizations to consolidate servers, optimize resource utilization, and improve flexibility and agility.

VMs offer isolation, flexibility, and resource allocation capabilities that make them suitable for a wide range of workloads and scenarios.

Whether used in on-premises data centers or cloud environments, virtualization remains a foundational technology in the world of IT, driving efficiency, cost savings, and innovation.

Auto Scaling and load balancing are essential techniques in modern cloud computing and data center environments, enabling organizations to maintain optimal performance, availability, and cost-efficiency for their applications and services.

Auto Scaling is a dynamic resource management strategy that automatically adjusts the number of compute resources allocated to an application or service based on predefined policies and rules.

This technique ensures that the application can handle varying workloads and traffic levels without manual intervention.

Auto Scaling is particularly valuable in cloud environments, where resources can be provisioned and deprovisioned rapidly to accommodate changing demands.

One of the primary benefits of Auto Scaling is cost optimization, as it allows organizations to pay only for the resources they need at any given moment.

By automatically scaling resources up during periods of high demand and down during periods of low demand, organizations can avoid overprovisioning and reduce infrastructure costs.

Auto Scaling policies are defined based on specific triggers, such as CPU utilization, network traffic, or custom metrics, to determine when to add or remove instances.

For example, when CPU utilization exceeds a certain threshold for a specified duration, Auto Scaling can trigger the addition of new instances to handle the increased load.

Auto Scaling groups are used to define and manage a collection of instances that share the same configuration and scaling policies.

These groups ensure that instances are launched and terminated automatically to maintain the desired number of running instances.

Auto Scaling also integrates with load balancing techniques to distribute incoming traffic evenly across multiple instances, enhancing application availability and fault tolerance.

Load balancing is a critical component of application architecture that distributes incoming network traffic across multiple servers, ensuring that no single server is overwhelmed by excessive traffic.

Load balancers can be implemented at various layers of the OSI model, including application layer, transport layer, and network layer, depending on the specific requirements of the application.

Application load balancers, for instance, operate at the application layer and can perform tasks such as SSL termination, content-based routing, and session persistence.

Network load balancers operate at the transport layer and distribute traffic at the IP level, making them suitable for handling high volumes of traffic efficiently.

Load balancing strategies can be divided into several types, including round-robin, least connections, IP hash, and weighted load balancing.

Round-robin load balancing distributes traffic evenly to each available instance in a cyclic manner, making it a simple and effective method for load distribution.

Least connections load balancing directs traffic to the instance with the fewest active connections, ensuring even distribution based on the current workload.

IP hash load balancing uses a hash function to map client IP addresses to specific instances, providing session persistence by consistently routing requests from the same client to the same instance.

Weighted load balancing allows administrators to assign different weights to instances, enabling fine-grained control over traffic distribution.

In cloud environments, load balancers can be elastic and automatically adjust their configuration to accommodate changes in the number of instances.

Load balancers are often combined with Auto Scaling groups to create dynamic and highly available architectures.

Auto Scaling groups ensure that the desired number of instances are running and healthy, while load balancers distribute traffic evenly across those instances.

This combination enhances the fault tolerance and scalability of applications.

Load balancing can also support advanced features like health checks, which periodically assess the health of instances and remove unhealthy instances from the pool to prevent them from receiving traffic.

In addition to distributing traffic among healthy instances, load balancers can also route traffic to instances in specific regions or availability zones, allowing for multi-region redundancy and disaster recovery.

To further enhance availability, organizations can use redundant load balancers that operate in an active-passive or active-active configuration.

Active-passive load balancers have a primary instance that handles traffic, with a secondary instance on standby to take over in case of a primary instance failure.

Active-active load balancers distribute traffic across multiple active instances simultaneously, providing load balancing and redundancy in one.

Auto Scaling and load balancing are not limited to web applications but can be applied to a wide range of services, including database servers, application servers, and microservices.

Load balancing techniques can also be used to distribute traffic among different regions or data centers, providing geographic redundancy and ensuring high availability even in the event of regional outages.

In summary, Auto Scaling and load balancing are essential techniques in modern cloud computing and data center environments.

Auto Scaling allows organizations to dynamically adjust resource allocation based on workload and traffic, optimizing cost efficiency and application performance.

Load balancing ensures that incoming traffic is evenly distributed across multiple instances, enhancing application availability, fault tolerance, and scalability.

By combining these techniques, organizations can build highly available and resilient architectures that can withstand fluctuations in traffic and provide a seamless experience to users.

Chapter 7: Security and Compliance in Cloud Infrastructure

Cloud security is a critical aspect of modern IT infrastructure, given the increasing reliance on cloud services for data storage, application hosting, and computing resources.

Ensuring the security of cloud-based assets is essential to protect sensitive data, maintain compliance with regulations, and prevent unauthorized access or data breaches.

Cloud security best practices encompass a range of strategies and measures to mitigate risks and maintain a secure cloud environment.

One of the foundational principles of cloud security is the principle of shared responsibility, which defines the division of security responsibilities between cloud service providers (CSPs) and customers.

CSPs are responsible for securing the underlying cloud infrastructure, including physical data centers, networks, and hardware.

Customers, on the other hand, are responsible for securing their data, applications, and configurations within the cloud.

This shared responsibility model emphasizes the need for customers to implement their own security controls and follow best practices to protect their cloud assets.

A crucial aspect of cloud security is identity and access management (IAM), which involves managing user identities and controlling their access to cloud resources.

Implementing strong authentication methods, such as multi-factor authentication (MFA), helps ensure that only authorized users can access cloud accounts and services.

IAM also includes role-based access control (RBAC) to define and manage permissions for different user roles within an organization.

Regularly reviewing and auditing IAM configurations to ensure they align with security policies is essential.

Data encryption is another critical component of cloud security, as it protects data both in transit and at rest.

Utilizing encryption protocols and services provided by CSPs, such as SSL/TLS for data in transit and encryption at rest for data stored in cloud databases or storage services, adds an additional layer of protection.

Customer-managed encryption keys can enhance control over data encryption.

Network security plays a vital role in cloud security by safeguarding traffic between cloud resources and the internet.

Implementing firewalls, intrusion detection systems (IDS), and intrusion prevention systems (IPS) can help monitor and protect against malicious network activity.

Segmenting cloud networks into isolated subnets or virtual private clouds (VPCs) can limit the exposure of critical resources and reduce the attack surface.

Regularly monitoring network traffic and conducting vulnerability assessments can help identify and mitigate potential security risks.

Cloud providers often offer security monitoring and alerting services that can assist in identifying and responding to security incidents.

Logging and auditing cloud activities and events are essential for detecting and investigating security breaches.

Collecting and analyzing logs from cloud services, including authentication and access logs, can provide insights into potentially suspicious activities.

Implementing a Security Information and Event Management (SIEM) system can centralize log management and automate threat detection.

Regularly reviewing and analyzing logs can help identify security incidents and enable timely responses.

Another key aspect of cloud security is compliance with relevant regulations and industry standards.

Ensuring that cloud deployments align with industry-specific compliance requirements, such as HIPAA for healthcare or PCI DSS for payment card data, is crucial.

Cloud providers often offer compliance resources and certification reports to assist customers in meeting their compliance goals.

Security patch management is vital to address known vulnerabilities and protect cloud resources from exploitation.

Regularly applying security patches and updates to cloud instances, operating systems, and software components helps mitigate the risk of security breaches.

Automated patch management tools can streamline this process and ensure timely updates.

Implementing a robust incident response plan is essential for addressing security incidents and breaches effectively.

This plan should include procedures for identifying, containing, eradicating, and recovering from security incidents.

Regularly conducting incident response drills and tabletop exercises can help ensure that the response team is prepared to handle various scenarios.

Security awareness and training programs are essential to educate employees and users about security best practices and threats specific to the cloud environment.

Employees should be aware of phishing attacks, social engineering attempts, and the importance of strong password management.

Security policies and procedures should be documented, communicated, and enforced throughout the organization to maintain a culture of security.

Cloud providers often offer a range of security tools and services that can enhance cloud security.

These services may include threat detection, identity management, encryption, and compliance management tools.

Leveraging these built-in security capabilities can help organizations meet their security requirements more efficiently.

Regularly assessing and validating the security of cloud configurations is crucial.

Conducting security assessments, penetration testing, and vulnerability scanning can help identify and remediate potential security weaknesses.

Cloud security best practices also involve backup and disaster recovery planning.

Regularly backing up data and creating disaster recovery plans can help organizations recover from data loss or service interruptions.

Testing disaster recovery plans and backups to ensure they are effective is essential.

As cloud environments evolve, it's important to stay informed about emerging threats and vulnerabilities.

Monitoring security advisories and updates from cloud providers, security organizations, and government agencies can help organizations proactively address security risks.

In summary, cloud security best practices are essential for safeguarding data, applications, and resources in cloud environments.

These practices encompass a wide range of measures, including IAM, encryption, network security, monitoring, compliance, patch management, incident response, training, and more.

By following these best practices and staying vigilant, organizations can maintain a secure and resilient cloud infrastructure that protects against evolving threats and vulnerabilities.

Regulatory compliance is a critical aspect of modern business operations, requiring organizations to adhere to laws, regulations, and industry standards that govern their activities.

These regulations are designed to protect consumers, ensure fair business practices, and maintain the integrity of financial markets.

In many industries, non-compliance with regulatory requirements can result in severe consequences, including fines, legal actions, damage to reputation, and loss of customer trust.

One of the primary challenges of regulatory compliance is the complexity of the regulatory landscape, with different regulations applying to specific industries and regions.

For example, the healthcare industry is subject to the Health Insurance Portability and Accountability Act (HIPAA), while financial institutions must comply with the Sarbanes-Oxley Act (SOX) and the Payment Card Industry Data Security Standard (PCI DSS).

Global organizations must also consider international regulations like the General Data Protection Regulation (GDPR) for data protection and privacy.

Compliance with these regulations requires a comprehensive understanding of the specific requirements and the ability to implement controls and processes that align with them.

Audit trails play a crucial role in regulatory compliance by providing a detailed record of activities, transactions, and events within an organization's systems and processes.

These audit trails serve as a valuable tool for demonstrating compliance with regulatory requirements and providing evidence of due diligence.

Audit trails capture information such as user access, data modifications, system configurations, and security events.

They record who performed specific actions, what those actions were, when they occurred, and the outcome of those actions.

In the context of regulatory compliance, audit trails are often used to track access to sensitive data, changes to financial records, and security incidents.

Implementing effective audit trails requires the use of logging mechanisms and security controls within IT systems and applications.

Modern organizations rely heavily on digital systems, making it essential to establish electronic audit trails that can be easily accessed, reviewed, and analyzed.

Audit trail data should be securely stored and protected from unauthorized tampering or deletion.

It is also important to establish clear retention policies for audit trail data to ensure compliance with data retention requirements specified by regulations.

Regulatory compliance often involves periodic audits and assessments by internal or external auditors.

During these audits, auditors examine an organization's processes, controls, and records to ensure they align with the applicable regulations.

Audit trails provide auditors with a detailed history of system and data activities, enabling them to verify compliance and identify any potential issues or violations.

Maintaining a comprehensive audit trail can streamline the auditing process and reduce the time and effort required to demonstrate compliance.

In some cases, regulatory authorities may require organizations to submit audit trail data as part of compliance reporting.

To meet these requirements, organizations must ensure that their audit trails are accurate, complete, and readily accessible for reporting purposes.

Furthermore, audit trails should be able to withstand scrutiny and verification by auditors or regulatory authorities.

One of the key benefits of audit trails is their role in enhancing transparency and accountability within organizations.

By recording and documenting all relevant activities and transactions, audit trails promote transparency by providing a clear and unbiased record of events.

This transparency helps organizations identify and address potential issues or irregularities, reducing the risk of fraud or misconduct.

In addition to regulatory compliance, audit trails also support internal investigations and incident response efforts.

When security incidents or data breaches occur, audit trails can provide valuable forensic evidence to help determine the cause, scope, and impact of the incident.

They can assist in identifying the parties involved and the steps taken to mitigate the incident.

By analyzing audit trail data, organizations can enhance their incident response processes and implement measures to prevent similar incidents in the future.

To maximize the effectiveness of audit trails for regulatory compliance, organizations should consider several best practices.

First, they should establish clear and well-documented policies and procedures for audit trail creation, retention, and access.

These policies should define the types of events and activities that should be logged, the retention periods for audit data, and the roles and responsibilities of personnel responsible for managing audit trails.

Second, organizations should implement robust logging and monitoring solutions that capture relevant events and activities across their IT infrastructure.

This includes server logs, database logs, application logs, network logs, and security event logs.

Third, organizations should regularly review and analyze audit trail data to identify patterns, anomalies, or potential compliance violations.

Automated log analysis tools and security information and event management (SIEM) systems can assist in this process by providing real-time monitoring and alerting capabilities.

Fourth, organizations should establish a secure and tamper-evident storage mechanism for audit trail data.

This may involve the use of secure, centralized log repositories, encryption, and access controls to protect the integrity and confidentiality of audit data.

Fifth, organizations should conduct periodic audits of their audit trails and associated processes to ensure that they remain effective and compliant with regulatory requirements.

Internal audits and assessments can help identify and address any gaps or weaknesses in audit trail management.

In summary, regulatory compliance is a critical consideration for organizations operating in various industries.

Audit trails play a vital role in demonstrating compliance with regulatory requirements by providing a comprehensive record of system and data activities.

By implementing effective audit trail management practices, organizations can enhance transparency, accountability, and security while reducing the risk of non-compliance and its associated consequences.

Chapter 8: Deploying and Managing Applications

Application deployment models in the cloud represent various strategies and approaches for hosting and running software applications within cloud computing environments. These models define how applications are provisioned, managed, and accessed, offering different levels of control, scalability, and flexibility to meet specific business requirements.

One of the most common cloud deployment models is the public cloud, where cloud providers make computing resources, such as virtual machines, storage, and networking, available to multiple customers over the internet.

Public clouds are operated and managed by third-party cloud service providers, and customers can access and use cloud resources on a pay-as-you-go basis.

Public cloud services offer high scalability, allowing organizations to quickly deploy and scale applications to meet changing demands.

They also provide a wide range of services and tools for application development, making it easier for developers to create and deploy applications.

Another deployment model is the private cloud, which is a cloud infrastructure dedicated to a single organization.

Private clouds can be hosted on-premises or by a third-party cloud provider and are designed to provide the same benefits as public clouds, such as scalability and self-service, but with more control and security.

Private clouds are often chosen by organizations with strict security and compliance requirements or those looking to maintain greater control over their infrastructure.

Hybrid cloud is a deployment model that combines elements of both public and private clouds, allowing data and applications to be shared between them.

This model enables organizations to take advantage of the scalability and cost-effectiveness of public clouds while maintaining sensitive data and critical applications in a private cloud.

Hybrid cloud deployments can be complex to manage but offer flexibility and adaptability.

Multi-cloud is an extension of the hybrid cloud model, where organizations use multiple cloud providers to host their applications and data.

This approach offers redundancy, resilience, and the ability to choose the best services from different providers for specific use cases.

Multi-cloud deployments require robust management and orchestration tools to ensure seamless integration between multiple cloud environments.

Serverless computing is a deployment model that abstracts the infrastructure entirely, allowing developers to focus solely on writing code.

In a serverless architecture, cloud providers automatically manage the provisioning and scaling of resources, and customers are billed based on the actual usage of their code.

This model simplifies application deployment and reduces operational overhead but requires developers to adopt a different mindset and design applications as a collection of stateless functions.

Containerization is a deployment model that involves packaging an application and its dependencies into a lightweight container, making it easy to deploy and run consistently across different environments.

Containers provide isolation and portability and are well-suited for microservices-based architectures.

Kubernetes, an open-source container orchestration platform, is commonly used to manage and deploy containerized applications in the cloud.

Edge computing is a deployment model that brings computation closer to the data source or end-user, reducing latency and improving performance for applications that require real-time processing.

Edge computing deployments involve deploying servers or computing resources in proximity to the edge devices or sensors, often in remote or distributed locations.

This model is used for applications like IoT, content delivery, and edge analytics.

Serverless edge computing combines the benefits of serverless and edge computing by allowing developers to deploy code to edge devices or nodes in a serverless manner.

This approach is particularly useful for applications that require low latency and offline capabilities in edge environments.

Cloud deployment models offer organizations various options for hosting and running their applications, each with its own advantages and trade-offs.

Choosing the right deployment model depends on factors such as scalability requirements, security concerns, regulatory compliance, and the nature of the applications being deployed.

By understanding these deployment models and their characteristics, organizations can make informed decisions about how to best leverage cloud computing to meet their business needs.

Containerization and orchestration tools have revolutionized the way software applications are developed, deployed, and managed in modern computing environments.

Containerization is a technology that allows applications and their dependencies to be packaged together in a standardized format called a container.

Containers are lightweight, portable, and can run consistently across different computing environments, making them an ideal solution for building, packaging, and deploying applications.

One of the most popular containerization technologies is Docker, which has gained widespread adoption in the software development community.

Docker containers encapsulate an application and its runtime dependencies, including libraries and configuration files, into a single package.

This packaging approach ensures that applications run reliably and consistently, regardless of the underlying infrastructure.

Containerization also promotes the use of microservices architecture, where applications are broken down into smaller, independently deployable components known as microservices.

Each microservice is packaged in its own container, allowing developers to build and scale individual components without affecting the entire application.

Container orchestration is the process of managing and automating the deployment, scaling, and operation of containerized applications.

Orchestration tools help organizations manage large-scale container deployments by providing features like automatic load balancing, scaling, and self-healing.

Kubernetes is the leading container orchestration platform, developed by Google and later open-sourced.

Kubernetes abstracts the underlying infrastructure and provides a declarative way to define the desired state of an application.

Operators can specify the number of desired replicas, resource requirements, and service dependencies, and Kubernetes ensures that the application runs as specified.

Kubernetes also offers features like rolling updates and canary deployments, allowing organizations to update applications without downtime or disruption.

Another popular container orchestration tool is Docker Swarm, which is included with Docker Enterprise.

Docker Swarm provides a simple and easy-to-use orchestration solution that is tightly integrated with Docker containers.

While not as feature-rich as Kubernetes, Docker Swarm is well-suited for smaller-scale deployments and organizations looking for a straightforward way to manage containerized applications.

Amazon Elastic Container Service (ECS) and Amazon Elastic Kubernetes Service (EKS) are container orchestration solutions offered by AWS.

ECS is a fully managed service that simplifies container deployment and scaling, while EKS provides a managed Kubernetes service for organizations that prefer to use Kubernetes.

Both services integrate seamlessly with other AWS services and provide features like automatic scaling, load balancing, and security.

Microsoft Azure offers Azure Kubernetes Service (AKS), a managed Kubernetes service that simplifies container orchestration in the Azure cloud environment.

AKS provides features like automatic scaling, monitoring, and integrated security, making it a suitable choice for organizations using Azure.

Google Cloud offers Google Kubernetes Engine (GKE), a managed Kubernetes service that is tightly integrated with Google Cloud Platform.

GKE provides advanced features like auto-scaling, cluster upgrades, and integrated logging and monitoring.

Container orchestration tools like Kubernetes, Docker Swarm, and cloud-specific services have become essential for organizations adopting containerization and microservices architectures.

These tools enable organizations to build, deploy, and manage containerized applications at scale, improving agility, efficiency, and reliability.

Container registries are repositories where container images are stored and managed.

They play a crucial role in the containerization and orchestration workflow, as container images need to be easily accessible and distributable to different environments.

Docker Hub is a popular public container registry that hosts a vast library of container images shared by the community.

Organizations can also set up private container registries, such as Docker Registry, to store and manage their proprietary container images.

These private registries provide control over access, security, and versioning of container images.

Container orchestration tools like Kubernetes and Docker Swarm interact with container registries to pull and deploy container images.

Continuous integration and continuous delivery (CI/CD) pipelines often integrate with container registries to automate the building and pushing of container images.

In addition to Docker Hub, other container registries like Google Container Registry, AWS Elastic Container Registry (ECR), and Azure Container Registry (ACR) are tightly integrated with their respective cloud platforms.

These cloud-specific registries offer features like IAM integration, image scanning, and tight integration with container orchestration services.

Container security is a critical aspect of containerization and orchestration.

Security best practices include regularly updating container images to patch vulnerabilities, scanning container images for security issues, implementing access controls, and using network segmentation to isolate containers.

Container runtime security solutions, like container firewalls and runtime protection tools, can further enhance container security.

Monitoring and logging are essential for gaining visibility into containerized applications and infrastructure.

Container orchestration platforms often include monitoring and logging solutions or integrate with third-party tools for this purpose.

Prometheus and Grafana are popular monitoring and visualization tools used in conjunction with Kubernetes for container monitoring.

Containerization and orchestration have become fundamental technologies for modern application development and deployment.

They offer scalability, portability, and automation that simplify the management of complex, distributed applications.

By understanding and effectively utilizing containerization and orchestration tools, organizations can optimize their software delivery pipelines, improve resource utilization, and enhance the reliability and security of their applications.

Chapter 9: High Availability and Disaster Recovery Strategies

High availability is a crucial consideration for organizations operating in cloud environments, as it ensures that their services and applications remain accessible and operational, even in the face of failures or disruptions.

Achieving high availability involves designing and implementing redundancy, fault tolerance, and disaster recovery strategies to minimize downtime and maintain service continuity.

Cloud service providers offer various tools and services to help organizations achieve high availability, but it's essential to understand the principles and best practices for designing resilient architectures.

One key concept in achieving high availability is redundancy, which involves duplicating critical components or resources to eliminate single points of failure.

Redundancy can be applied at various levels, including hardware, networking, and software, to ensure that if one component fails, another can seamlessly take over.

In cloud environments, redundancy can be achieved by deploying resources across multiple availability zones or regions provided by the cloud provider.

An availability zone is a separate, physically isolated data center with its own power, cooling, and networking infrastructure.

By distributing resources across availability zones, organizations can ensure that their services remain available even if one zone experiences an outage.

In addition to redundancy, load balancing is another fundamental component of high availability.

Load balancers distribute incoming network traffic across multiple instances or servers to ensure that no single resource becomes overwhelmed.

Cloud providers offer load balancing services that can automatically distribute traffic to healthy instances, preventing overloads and ensuring consistent service availability.

Failover mechanisms are essential for high availability, as they enable the automatic transition of operations from a failed resource to a backup resource.

For example, in a database cluster, if one database node fails, a failover mechanism can promote a standby node to become the primary node, ensuring uninterrupted database access.

Cloud providers offer managed database services with built-in failover capabilities to simplify this process.

To achieve high availability in cloud environments, organizations should also consider data replication and backup strategies.

Data replication involves copying data to multiple locations, ensuring that if one copy becomes inaccessible or corrupted, another copy is readily available.

Cloud providers offer replication features for storage and databases, allowing organizations to replicate data across different geographic regions for redundancy.

Regular backups of critical data are essential for disaster recovery and ensuring data availability in case of data corruption, deletion, or other issues.

Cloud providers offer backup and snapshot services that can automate the backup process and enable the restoration of data to a previous state.

High availability architectures often involve the use of auto-scaling, a capability that automatically adjusts the number of resources in response to changes in demand.

Auto-scaling can help organizations ensure that their services remain responsive during peak usage periods and can scale down to save costs during periods of lower demand.

To effectively implement auto-scaling, organizations need to monitor resource utilization and set up triggers to initiate scaling actions based on predefined criteria.

Another important aspect of high availability is disaster recovery planning, which involves preparing for and mitigating the impact of catastrophic events or large-scale failures.

Cloud providers offer disaster recovery services, such as backup and replication, to help organizations replicate data and applications to a secondary location.

Implementing a disaster recovery plan that includes regular testing and validation is crucial to ensuring that organizations can recover quickly in the event of a disaster.

Cloud providers also offer geographic redundancy, allowing organizations to deploy resources in multiple regions or data centers to minimize the impact of regional outages.

Organizations should assess their risk tolerance and regulatory requirements to determine the appropriate level of geographic redundancy needed for their applications.

Monitoring and alerting are essential components of high availability, as they provide visibility into the health and performance of cloud resources.

Cloud providers offer monitoring and alerting services that can track the status of resources, generate alerts for predefined events, and trigger automated responses.

Effective monitoring and alerting allow organizations to identify and address potential issues before they impact service availability.

High availability in the cloud also requires robust security practices.

Organizations should implement security measures, such as network segmentation, access controls, and encryption, to protect their resources and data from threats.

Regular security assessments, vulnerability scanning, and penetration testing can help identify and remediate potential security weaknesses.

Lastly, achieving high availability in the cloud requires continuous testing and validation of resilience strategies.

Organizations should conduct regular tests and drills to ensure that their redundancy, failover, and disaster recovery mechanisms function as expected.

These tests help identify any weaknesses in the high availability architecture and allow organizations to make necessary improvements.

In summary, achieving high availability in cloud environments is a critical objective for organizations seeking to deliver reliable and uninterrupted services.

High availability involves redundancy, load balancing, failover mechanisms, data replication, backup strategies, auto-scaling, disaster recovery planning, geographic redundancy, monitoring and alerting, security measures, and continuous testing.

By implementing these principles and best practices, organizations can ensure that their cloud-based applications and services remain accessible and operational, even in the face of failures and disruptions, ultimately delivering a seamless and reliable experience to their users.

Disaster recovery planning is a critical aspect of ensuring the continuity of business operations in the face of unexpected events or disasters that can disrupt IT systems and infrastructure.

These events can include natural disasters like earthquakes, hurricanes, or floods, as well as human-made incidents such as cyberattacks, hardware failures, or power outages.

A well-thought-out disaster recovery plan helps organizations minimize downtime, protect data, and recover quickly in the event of a disaster.

One key component of disaster recovery planning is understanding the concept of Recovery Time Objective (RTO) and Recovery Point Objective (RPO).

RTO represents the maximum acceptable downtime for a system or application, indicating how quickly it should be back up and running after a disaster.

RPO represents the maximum acceptable data loss, indicating how much data an organization is willing to lose in the event of a disaster.

The choice of RTO and RPO values is crucial, as it guides the selection of appropriate disaster recovery solutions and strategies.

Failover solutions are a fundamental part of disaster recovery planning, as they enable the seamless transition of operations from a failed system or location to a backup system or location.

Failover mechanisms can be implemented at various levels, including hardware, networking, and software.

Hardware failover solutions involve redundant hardware components, such as servers, storage, and network devices, that automatically take over when the primary hardware fails.

Redundant power supplies, hot-swappable components, and clustering are common techniques used for hardware failover.

Network failover solutions ensure network connectivity remains available in the event of network failures.

These solutions can include redundant network paths, load balancing, and failover routers or switches.

Software failover solutions focus on application-level failover, where redundant software instances or virtual machines automatically take over when the primary instance fails.

These solutions often require specialized software and configurations to detect failures and trigger failover events.

Cloud computing has introduced new opportunities and challenges for disaster recovery planning and failover solutions.

Cloud-based disaster recovery solutions offer scalability, flexibility, and cost-effectiveness compared to traditional on-premises solutions.

One approach to cloud-based disaster recovery is to replicate critical systems and data to the cloud, enabling rapid recovery in case of an on-premises disaster.

Cloud providers offer disaster recovery services that facilitate the replication of data and applications to geographically dispersed data centers, ensuring redundancy and availability.

Failover to the cloud involves redirecting user traffic and operations to cloud-based resources when on-premises systems are unavailable.

This approach leverages the cloud's elasticity and geographic redundancy to maintain service availability.

Hybrid cloud architectures combine on-premises infrastructure with cloud resources, offering a flexible and adaptable disaster recovery strategy.

In a hybrid cloud model, organizations can use the cloud for backup and failover while retaining critical systems and data on-premises.

This approach provides the benefits of cloud-based disaster recovery while accommodating specific security or compliance requirements.

Public cloud providers, such as Amazon Web Services (AWS), Microsoft Azure, and Google Cloud Platform (GCP), offer a range of disaster recovery services and tools.

For example, AWS offers Amazon S3 for data storage and Amazon EC2 instances for compute resources to support disaster recovery.

Microsoft Azure provides Azure Site Recovery for replicating on-premises workloads to Azure and Azure Traffic Manager for global load balancing and failover.

Google Cloud offers Cloud Storage for data storage and Google Compute Engine for scalable compute resources.

To ensure a successful disaster recovery strategy, organizations must perform regular testing and validation of their failover solutions.

Testing helps identify any issues or gaps in the recovery process and allows organizations to refine their plans and procedures.

Automated failover testing tools can simulate failover events without impacting production systems, ensuring that failover mechanisms function as expected.

Documentation of disaster recovery plans and procedures is essential for guiding personnel during recovery efforts.

Clear and detailed documentation should include step-by-step instructions for initiating failover, contacting relevant personnel, and verifying the success of the recovery process.

Regular training and drills involving IT staff and other stakeholders can ensure that everyone is familiar with their roles and responsibilities in a disaster recovery scenario.

Finally, communication and coordination are critical during disaster recovery efforts.

Organizations should establish communication plans that outline how and when stakeholders will be notified of a disaster and how updates will be provided throughout the recovery process.

Coordination between IT teams, management, and external partners is essential to ensure a cohesive and effective response.

In summary, disaster recovery planning and failover solutions are essential components of an organization's overall business continuity strategy.

Understanding Recovery Time Objective (RTO) and Recovery Point Objective (RPO) is crucial for setting appropriate recovery goals.

Failover solutions, whether hardware, network, or software-based, play a central role in achieving rapid recovery and minimizing downtime.

Cloud-based disaster recovery solutions provide scalability and flexibility, while hybrid cloud architectures offer a balance between on-premises and cloud resources.

Regular testing, documentation, training, and communication are key elements of a successful disaster recovery plan.

By investing in comprehensive disaster recovery planning and effective failover solutions, organizations can ensure business continuity and resilience in the face of unforeseen disasters and disruptions.

Chapter 10: Optimization and Cost Management Techniques

Cost analysis and optimization strategies are essential for organizations to manage their cloud expenses effectively and ensure they are getting the most value from their cloud investments.

In a cloud environment, organizations pay for the resources they consume, making it crucial to understand and control costs to avoid unexpected expenses.

One fundamental aspect of cost analysis is understanding cloud pricing models, which can vary among cloud providers.

Cloud providers typically offer multiple pricing models, including pay-as-you-go, reserved instances, and spot instances, each with its own pricing structure and trade-offs.

Pay-as-you-go pricing allows organizations to pay only for the resources they use, offering flexibility but potentially leading to higher costs if resources are not carefully managed.

Reserved instances offer cost savings in exchange for a commitment to a specific instance type and duration, making them a cost-effective option for predictable workloads.

Spot instances provide steep discounts on unused capacity but may be terminated with little notice, making them suitable for fault-tolerant or batch processing workloads.

To perform effective cost analysis, organizations should regularly monitor their cloud spending and resource utilization.

Cloud providers offer cost management tools and dashboards that provide visibility into spending trends and resource usage.

By analyzing this data, organizations can identify cost outliers, underutilized resources, and opportunities for cost optimization.

Resource tagging is a valuable practice that enables organizations to categorize and track cloud resources based on their purpose, owner, or department.

Tagging allows for more granular cost allocation and helps organizations identify the cost drivers for specific projects or teams.

Cost allocation reports generated based on tags can facilitate chargebacks or showbacks to internal departments, promoting cost accountability.

Rightsizing is a key cost optimization strategy that involves matching cloud resources to actual workload requirements.

Over-provisioning resources can lead to unnecessary costs, while under-provisioning can result in performance issues.

Rightsizing requires continuous monitoring and adjustment of resource allocations to ensure they align with workload demands.

Cloud providers offer tools and recommendations to help organizations identify opportunities for rightsizing, such as AWS Trusted Advisor or Azure Cost Management.

Reserved instances (RIs) and savings plans are cost optimization options that can significantly reduce cloud expenses.

By committing to a specific instance type and term, organizations can benefit from significant discounts compared to pay-as-you-go pricing.

Reserved instances are ideal for workloads with predictable usage patterns, while savings plans offer more flexibility for a broader range of instance types.

Using auto-scaling and elasticity features can help organizations optimize costs by automatically adjusting resources to match workload demands.

Auto-scaling allows cloud resources to dynamically scale up or down in response to changing traffic or resource utilization.

By setting appropriate scaling policies, organizations can ensure that resources are neither underutilized nor overprovisioned, optimizing costs while maintaining performance.

Storage optimization is another critical aspect of cost analysis and optimization.

Organizations can reduce storage costs by regularly reviewing and deleting outdated data, leveraging storage tiering options, and enabling data lifecycle policies to automatically move data to lower-cost storage classes.

Cost analysis and optimization should also consider network costs, as data transfer and egress charges can add up.

Optimizing network costs involves minimizing unnecessary data transfer and choosing the right network architecture to reduce latency and costs.

In addition to cloud-specific cost management tools, organizations can benefit from third-party cost optimization solutions and services.

These tools offer advanced analytics, automation, and recommendations for optimizing cloud costs based on best practices and historical data.

Cloud cost governance is an essential practice for managing cloud expenses.

It involves establishing policies, guidelines, and approval processes for cloud resource provisioning.

Effective governance ensures that cloud resources are provisioned and used in line with organizational objectives and budget constraints.

Cloud providers offer cost budgeting and forecasting tools to help organizations set and track spending limits, enabling proactive cost management.

Cost analysis and optimization is an ongoing process that requires continuous monitoring and adjustment.

Regularly reviewing cost reports, rightsizing resources, optimizing storage, and implementing cost-saving strategies are essential for maintaining control over cloud expenses.

In summary, cost analysis and optimization strategies are essential for organizations operating in the cloud.

Understanding cloud pricing models, monitoring spending and resource utilization, and implementing cost-saving strategies are key to managing cloud costs effectively.

Resource tagging, rightsizing, and the use of reserved instances or savings plans can lead to significant cost savings.

Auto-scaling, storage optimization, and network cost management are additional considerations in the pursuit of cost optimization.

Cloud cost governance and the use of third-party cost optimization tools can further enhance an organization's ability to manage cloud expenses and ensure that cloud investments are aligned with business objectives.

Cloud cost management tools and practices are essential for organizations to control and optimize their spending in cloud environments, where resource consumption can quickly lead to unexpected expenses.

Cloud cost management encompasses a range of activities and strategies aimed at understanding, tracking, and controlling cloud expenses.

Effective cost management enables organizations to maximize the value they derive from their cloud investments while staying within budgetary constraints.

One of the foundational practices of cloud cost management is tracking and monitoring cloud spending.

Cloud providers offer cost management tools and dashboards that provide visibility into spending trends, resource usage, and cost breakdowns.

By regularly reviewing these reports, organizations can gain insights into their cloud expenses and identify areas where optimization is needed.

Resource tagging is a valuable practice in cloud cost management, allowing organizations to categorize and track cloud resources based on their purpose, owner, department, or project.

Tagging provides more granular visibility into cost allocation and helps organizations understand which resources are driving specific costs.

Cost allocation reports generated based on tags can be used for internal chargebacks or showbacks, promoting accountability and cost awareness among different teams or departments.

Rightsizing is a key cost optimization strategy that involves matching cloud resources to actual workload requirements.

Over-provisioning resources can lead to unnecessary costs, while under-provisioning can result in performance issues.

Rightsizing requires continuous monitoring of resource utilization and adjusting resource allocations to align with workload demands.

Cloud providers offer tools and recommendations to help organizations identify opportunities for rightsizing, such as AWS Trusted Advisor or Azure Cost Management.

Reserved instances (RIs) and savings plans are cost optimization options that offer significant cost savings compared to pay-as-you-go pricing.

By committing to a specific instance type and term, organizations can benefit from substantial discounts.

Reserved instances are well-suited for workloads with predictable usage patterns, while savings plans offer more flexibility by applying savings to a broader range of instance types.

Auto-scaling and elasticity features are essential for optimizing costs in cloud environments.

Auto-scaling allows cloud resources to dynamically adjust to changing traffic or resource utilization, ensuring that resources are neither underutilized nor overprovisioned.

Properly configured auto-scaling policies help organizations optimize costs while maintaining performance.

Storage optimization is another critical aspect of cloud cost management.

Organizations can reduce storage costs by regularly reviewing and deleting outdated data, leveraging storage tiering options, and enabling data lifecycle policies to automatically move data to lower-cost storage classes.

Network costs, including data transfer and egress charges, should also be considered in cloud cost management.

Optimizing network costs involves minimizing unnecessary data transfer and selecting the right network architecture to reduce latency and costs.

Effective cost management in the cloud requires proactive budgeting and forecasting.

Cloud providers offer budgeting and forecasting tools that help organizations set and track spending limits, enabling them to stay within budget constraints.

Third-party cost optimization solutions and services can complement cloud providers' tools by offering advanced analytics, automation, and recommendations based on best practices and historical data.

Cost governance is an essential aspect of cloud cost management, involving the establishment of policies, guidelines, and approval processes for cloud resource provisioning.

Effective governance ensures that cloud resources are provisioned and used in alignment with organizational objectives and budgetary constraints.

Regular cost reviews and optimization efforts are essential in the pursuit of effective cloud cost management.

By continuously monitoring cost reports, rightsizing resources, optimizing storage, and implementing cost-saving strategies, organizations can maintain control over their cloud expenses.

Auto-scaling, storage optimization, and network cost management are additional considerations that can contribute to cost optimization.

Cloud cost governance, along with third-party cost optimization tools, enhances an organization's ability to manage cloud expenses effectively and ensure that cloud investments are aligned with business goals.

In summary, cloud cost management is a critical discipline for organizations leveraging cloud computing.

It involves practices such as tracking and monitoring spending, resource tagging, rightsizing, and the use of reserved instances or savings plans.

Auto-scaling, storage optimization, and network cost management also play significant roles in cost optimization.

Effective cost governance and the use of third-party cost optimization tools are essential components of a comprehensive approach to cloud cost management.

Book 3
Advanced IaaS Architectures
Optimizing Microsoft Azure for Enterprises

ROB BOTWRIGHT

Chapter 1: The Role of Azure IaaS in Enterprise Solutions

Azure, Microsoft's cloud computing platform, has had a profound impact on modern enterprises and their ability to leverage the full potential of cloud technology.

As businesses increasingly rely on digital solutions and data-driven decision-making, Azure has emerged as a versatile and powerful platform that addresses a wide range of enterprise needs.

One of the primary ways Azure has influenced modern enterprises is by providing a scalable and cost-effective infrastructure for hosting applications and services.

With Azure's vast data center network, organizations can quickly provision and scale resources to meet fluctuating demand without the upfront capital expenses associated with traditional on-premises infrastructure.

This scalability allows businesses to respond rapidly to changing market conditions and customer demands, fostering agility and competitiveness.

Azure's infrastructure services, such as virtual machines, storage, and networking, enable organizations to build and deploy a wide variety of applications and workloads.

From web applications and databases to machine learning models and IoT solutions, Azure's infrastructure offerings provide the foundation for modern enterprise IT.

Furthermore, Azure's global reach and network connectivity make it possible for organizations to deploy applications closer to their customers, improving latency and user experience.

Azure's impact on modern enterprises also extends to data management and analytics.

Azure provides a robust ecosystem of data services and tools, including Azure SQL Database, Azure Cosmos DB, and Azure Data Lake Storage, that enable organizations to store, process, and analyze vast amounts of data with ease.

These services support both structured and unstructured data, making it possible for enterprises to gain insights from their data to drive better decision-making.

Azure's integration with popular data analytics and machine learning tools, such as Azure Machine Learning and Azure Databricks, empowers data scientists and analysts to build predictive models and extract valuable insights from data.

In addition to infrastructure and data capabilities, Azure has transformed application development practices for modern enterprises.

Azure DevOps services provide a comprehensive set of tools for agile software development, continuous integration, and continuous delivery (CI/CD).

These practices enable organizations to accelerate the development and deployment of software applications while maintaining high quality and reliability.

Azure also supports containerization and orchestration with Azure Kubernetes Service (AKS), allowing enterprises to build, deploy, and manage containerized applications at scale.

This approach fosters greater consistency and portability across different environments, from development to production.

Azure's impact on modern enterprises is further exemplified by its commitment to hybrid and multi-cloud scenarios.

Azure Arc extends Azure management and services to on-premises environments and other cloud providers, giving organizations a unified management experience and the flexibility to run workloads where it makes the most sense for their business.

This hybrid approach helps modern enterprises leverage existing investments in on-premises infrastructure while taking advantage of Azure's cloud-native capabilities.

Azure's identity and access management services, such as Azure Active Directory, enhance security and simplify user authentication and authorization for modern enterprises.

With Azure AD, organizations can implement single sign-on, multi-factor authentication, and role-based access control to protect their applications and data.

Additionally, Azure Security Center provides a comprehensive set of tools and recommendations for threat protection, helping enterprises safeguard their cloud resources from security threats and vulnerabilities.

Azure's impact on modern enterprises is also evident in its support for Internet of Things (IoT) solutions.

Azure IoT Hub and Azure IoT Central offer scalable and secure platforms for connecting, monitoring, and managing IoT devices and assets.

These services enable organizations to harness the power of IoT to improve operational efficiency, enhance customer experiences, and create new revenue streams.

Azure's commitment to sustainability and environmental responsibility aligns with the values and priorities of modern enterprises.

Microsoft has made significant investments in renewable energy and sustainability initiatives, including a commitment to be carbon negative by 2030.

By choosing Azure as their cloud platform, enterprises can contribute to a more sustainable future while benefiting from a responsible and environmentally conscious partner.

In summary, Azure's impact on modern enterprises is multifaceted and far-reaching.

It provides the essential infrastructure, data management, and application development capabilities that empower organizations to thrive in today's digital economy.

Azure's support for hybrid and multi-cloud scenarios, identity and access management, security, IoT, and sustainability further solidify its role as a transformative force in modern enterprise technology.

As businesses continue to evolve and embrace digital transformation, Azure's influence on modern enterprises is likely to grow, helping them innovate, compete, and succeed in an increasingly dynamic and data-driven world.

Leveraging Azure Infrastructure as a Service (IaaS) can be a pivotal step for organizations seeking to undergo meaningful business transformation.

In today's rapidly evolving digital landscape, businesses are constantly challenged to adapt, innovate, and remain competitive, and Azure IaaS offers a robust set of tools and capabilities to support these endeavors.

One of the key drivers for adopting Azure IaaS is the agility it provides to modern enterprises.

With traditional on-premises infrastructure, businesses often face lengthy procurement cycles, hardware constraints, and resource limitations that hinder their ability to respond quickly to changing market demands.

Azure IaaS eliminates these barriers by offering a cloud-based infrastructure that can be provisioned and scaled within minutes, enabling organizations to swiftly deploy new applications, expand their IT resources, and pivot to address emerging opportunities.

The ability to rapidly provision and scale resources empowers businesses to experiment, innovate, and iterate more effectively.

Azure IaaS offers a diverse range of virtual machines (VMs) with various configurations, enabling organizations to select the right compute power and memory capacity for their specific workloads.

This flexibility allows businesses to optimize performance and cost according to their unique needs, reducing the risk of over-provisioning or underutilization of resources.

In addition to agility and scalability, Azure IaaS enhances business continuity and disaster recovery capabilities.

Traditional disaster recovery solutions often involve maintaining secondary data centers, which can be costly and resource-intensive.

Azure's geographically dispersed data centers and replication options make it an attractive choice for ensuring the availability and resilience of critical systems and data.

Azure Site Recovery, for example, allows organizations to replicate on-premises workloads to Azure, providing a cost-effective and reliable disaster recovery solution.

Moreover, Azure's global network of data centers ensures that businesses can maintain operations even in the face of regional outages or disruptions.

Azure IaaS also facilitates cost savings and optimization by shifting from capital expenditure (CapEx) to operational expenditure (OpEx).

By eliminating the need to purchase and maintain physical hardware, businesses can reduce upfront costs and achieve predictable, pay-as-you-go pricing with Azure.

This financial flexibility allows organizations to allocate resources more efficiently, adapt to changing budget constraints, and allocate spending where it provides the most value.

Furthermore, Azure's cost management tools and recommendations help businesses identify opportunities for optimization, such as rightsizing VMs, leveraging reserved instances, and implementing auto-scaling policies to match resource consumption with demand.

Another transformative aspect of Azure IaaS is its role in enabling businesses to modernize their applications and infrastructure.

Legacy systems and monolithic applications can hinder innovation and hinder an organization's ability to respond to market shifts.

Azure provides a platform for modernization efforts, allowing businesses to containerize existing applications, refactor them to use microservices architecture, or rehost them in Azure VMs.

This modernization process not only improves agility and scalability but also enhances the overall efficiency of applications, reducing maintenance efforts and enabling faster development cycles.

Azure IaaS also plays a vital role in fostering a hybrid and multi-cloud strategy for business transformation.

Many organizations have existing investments in on-premises infrastructure, and Azure's hybrid capabilities, such as Azure Arc, extend Azure services and management to on-premises environments.

This approach allows businesses to leverage Azure's cloud-native tools and services while maintaining compatibility with their existing infrastructure.

By embracing a hybrid and multi-cloud strategy, organizations can maximize flexibility, avoid vendor lock-in, and choose the best deployment model for each workload.

Security and compliance are paramount concerns in the modern business landscape, and Azure IaaS offers robust solutions to address these challenges.

Azure's security services, such as Azure Security Center and Azure Sentinel, provide advanced threat protection, security monitoring, and compliance reporting.

Businesses can implement identity and access management controls through Azure Active Directory, ensuring secure user authentication and authorization.

Azure also provides compliance certifications and adheres to global regulatory standards, making it a trusted choice for organizations in highly regulated industries.

Finally, Azure IaaS serves as a catalyst for innovation by providing access to cutting-edge technologies and capabilities.

Organizations can harness Azure's extensive ecosystem of services, including artificial intelligence (AI), machine learning, Internet of Things (IoT), and blockchain, to develop innovative solutions that drive business growth and differentiation.

Azure's commitment to sustainability and environmental responsibility aligns with the values and priorities of modern enterprises.

By choosing Azure as their cloud platform, organizations can contribute to a more sustainable future while benefiting from a responsible and environmentally conscious partner.

In summary, leveraging Azure IaaS is a strategic imperative for organizations seeking meaningful business transformation.

The agility, scalability, business continuity, cost optimization, modernization, hybrid and multi-cloud capabilities, security, compliance, and innovation that Azure IaaS provides are essential enablers of a successful transformation journey.

As businesses continue to adapt and evolve in a rapidly changing world, Azure IaaS stands as a powerful ally, empowering them to embrace the future with confidence, agility, and innovation.

Chapter 2: Azure Infrastructure Components and Services

Understanding Azure resource groups and the resources they contain is fundamental to effectively managing and organizing your assets in the Azure cloud environment.

Azure resource groups serve as logical containers that help you group and manage related resources together, making it easier to organize, monitor, and manage your cloud infrastructure.

A resource group can be thought of as a way to organize various Azure resources, such as virtual machines, storage accounts, databases, and networking components, that are part of a single application, project, or environment.

Resource groups provide a way to define the scope for applying access control, monitoring, and billing.

When you create a resource group, you need to specify a name and the Azure region where you want to create it.

It's important to choose a name that reflects the purpose or function of the resource group, as it will help you and your team identify its contents later.

Once a resource group is created, you can add or remove resources from it as needed.

Resource groups offer several advantages when it comes to managing your Azure resources.

One of the key benefits is that resource groups allow you to manage the resources as a single entity.

This means you can start, stop, delete, or perform other management operations on all the resources within a resource group simultaneously.

Resource groups also help with access control and security management.

You can assign role-based access control (RBAC) permissions to resource groups, allowing you to grant specific individuals or teams the necessary permissions to manage the resources within the group.

This fine-grained control ensures that only authorized personnel can make changes to the resources.

Resource groups are also important for billing and cost management.

Azure tracks usage and costs at the resource group level, making it easier to understand and allocate costs for a particular project or department.

By organizing resources into separate resource groups, you can better track and manage your cloud spending.

Resource groups can be created and managed using various methods.

You can create resource groups through the Azure portal, Azure PowerShell, Azure CLI, Azure Resource Manager templates, or even Azure SDKs and REST APIs.

The choice of method depends on your preferences and automation needs.

Resource groups can contain a wide variety of Azure resources, depending on your application or project requirements.

Common resource types that you might find in a resource group include virtual machines, virtual networks, storage accounts, databases, web apps, and more.

Resource groups are not limited to containing resources of a single type; you can mix and match resources to suit your needs.

When it comes to naming conventions for resource groups, it's a good practice to use descriptive and meaningful names. For example, if you're creating a resource group for a web application, you could name it "MyWebAppResourceGroup" to clearly indicate its purpose.

Avoid using generic or ambiguous names that could lead to confusion later.

Resource groups also play a role in managing the lifecycle of resources.

When you delete a resource group, all the resources within it are also deleted.

This can be a convenient way to clean up and remove resources that are no longer needed.

However, it's essential to exercise caution when deleting resource groups, as this action is irreversible, and you could lose valuable data if not careful.

Resource groups can be nested within other resource groups, creating a hierarchy of resource group relationships.

This nesting can be useful for organizing resources at various levels, such as by department, project, or environment.

Each resource group within a hierarchy can have its own access control, monitoring, and billing settings, providing flexibility in resource management.

Resource groups also have associated metadata, including tags, that you can use to annotate and categorize your resource groups.

Tags allow you to add custom metadata to resource groups, making it easier to search, filter, and organize your resources based on specific criteria.

Tags can be especially valuable for tracking resources by project, owner, cost center, or other relevant attributes.

In summary, Azure resource groups are a fundamental concept for organizing and managing your Azure resources effectively.

They provide a logical container for grouping related resources, simplifying management tasks, and improving access control, billing, and cost management.

Resource groups offer flexibility in how you structure and organize your cloud infrastructure, making it easier to adapt to changing business needs and requirements.

Understanding how to create, manage, and utilize resource groups is essential for successful Azure resource management.

Configuring Azure Virtual Networks and Subnets is a fundamental aspect of designing and managing a network infrastructure in the Azure cloud environment.

Azure Virtual Network (VNet) is a logically isolated network within the Azure cloud that allows you to securely connect Azure resources to each other and to on-premises networks or the internet.

When setting up a VNet, you need to define its address space, which is a range of private IP addresses that your resources can use.

Choosing an appropriate address space is critical, as it affects IP address allocation and routing within the VNet.

Address spaces can be customized based on your specific requirements, but it's essential to avoid overlapping with other networks to prevent routing conflicts.

Once you have defined the address space, you can create subnets within the VNet.

Subnets allow you to further segment the address space into smaller, manageable segments, each serving a specific purpose or workload.

For example, you might create separate subnets for web servers, application servers, and databases to isolate and control traffic flow.

Each subnet has its address range, which is a subset of the VNet's address space.

Subnet addressing should be carefully planned to accommodate the expected number of resources and their respective IP requirements.

Azure Virtual Networks support both IPv4 and IPv6 addressing, providing flexibility for different scenarios and future-proofing your network.

When configuring subnets, you should also consider network security and access controls.

Azure provides Network Security Groups (NSGs) that allow you to define inbound and outbound security rules to filter and control network traffic at the subnet level.

NSGs are a critical component of network security in Azure and help protect your resources from unauthorized access and threats.

Additionally, Azure Firewall and Azure DDoS Protection provide advanced security features to safeguard your network and resources against cyberattacks.

Once you have designed and configured your VNet and subnets, you can establish connectivity between on-premises networks and Azure using various methods.

Azure VPN Gateway and Azure ExpressRoute are two common options for creating secure, high-performance connections to Azure.

Azure VPN Gateway provides site-to-site VPN connectivity over the internet, allowing on-premises networks to communicate securely with resources in Azure.

Azure ExpressRoute, on the other hand, offers dedicated private connections through a network service provider, providing a more reliable and consistent connection experience.

Virtual network peering is another feature that enables communication between VNets within the same region, simplifying network architecture and resource management.

Peered VNets can communicate with each other as if they were on the same network, making it easier to connect resources across multiple VNets.

Traffic between peered VNets remains on Microsoft's backbone network, ensuring low-latency and secure communication.

Azure also supports global VNet peering, which allows VNets in different Azure regions to connect seamlessly, enabling multi-region network architectures.

VNet peering does not require a gateway or additional hardware, making it a cost-effective and scalable solution.

Additionally, Azure Bastion is a secure and convenient way to access virtual machines within your VNets through Remote Desktop Protocol (RDP) or Secure Shell (SSH) without exposing them to the public internet.

It simplifies remote access management by providing a secure jump server within your VNet.

IP address management and allocation are essential considerations when configuring VNets and subnets.

Azure provides several options for IP address assignment, including dynamic and static assignment.

Dynamic IP assignment is the default option, where Azure automatically assigns IP addresses to resources within a subnet from a specified address range.

Static IP assignment allows you to reserve specific IP addresses for critical resources that require a consistent address, such as DNS servers or load balancers.

Effective IP address management is critical for maintaining network integrity and ensuring that resources can communicate without conflicts.

Azure offers features like Azure DNS for domain name resolution within VNets and Azure Private DNS for custom DNS configurations.

By integrating with Azure DNS, you can simplify DNS management and improve the overall performance and reliability of your network.

Traffic routing and routing tables are crucial components of VNet and subnet configuration.

Azure uses a built-in system of routes and routing tables to determine how traffic is directed within and between VNets.

By default, Azure provides system routes that handle most common routing scenarios.

However, you can also create custom routes and routing tables to control traffic flow more precisely.

Custom routes allow you to specify the next hop for specific destination IP ranges, enabling advanced routing configurations.

Additionally, route propagation and route tables can be used to control how routes are advertised and propagated between VNets and on-premises networks.

Network monitoring and diagnostics are essential for maintaining the health and performance of your Azure network infrastructure.

Azure Monitor and Azure Network Watcher are tools that provide insights and troubleshooting capabilities.

Azure Monitor helps you collect and analyze telemetry data from your VNets, enabling you to monitor network traffic, performance, and security.

Azure Network Watcher offers diagnostic and troubleshooting features, including packet capture, flow logs, and connection troubleshooting, to identify and resolve network issues.

In summary, Azure Virtual Network and Subnet configuration is a foundational element of designing and managing network infrastructure in the Azure cloud.

Careful planning of address spaces, subnets, security controls, and connectivity options is essential for creating a secure, scalable, and well-organized network environment.

By understanding the principles of VNet and subnet configuration, you can build robust and efficient network architectures to support your Azure workloads and applications effectively.

Chapter 3: Designing High-Performance Networks in Azure

Azure network topologies and best practices play a vital role in designing a robust and secure cloud infrastructure that can meet the demands of modern applications and workloads.

When designing an Azure network topology, it's crucial to consider factors such as scalability, security, and performance.

Azure offers several network topology options to accommodate different use cases, and choosing the right one is essential to achieving your specific goals.

One common network topology in Azure is the hub-and-spoke model, which provides a centralized hub network connected to multiple spoke networks.

The hub serves as a central point for network traffic and connectivity, while the spokes represent isolated environments or business units.

This topology simplifies network management and reduces the complexity of configuring and managing multiple connections.

It also allows for better control and monitoring of traffic flow between spokes through the hub.

Azure Virtual WAN is a service that simplifies hub-and-spoke network topology implementation by providing a managed, cloud-native solution for connecting branch offices and remote users to Azure.

Virtual WAN streamlines connectivity and routing, making it easier to set up and manage global network architectures.

Another important network topology in Azure is the VNet-to-VNet connection, which enables communication between virtual networks.

This topology is valuable for scenarios where different VNets need to interact while maintaining their isolation.

For example, you might have separate VNets for development, testing, and production environments, and VNet-to-VNet connections can facilitate secure communication between them.

Azure also offers the option to create global networks using the Global VNet Peering feature, which allows VNets in different Azure regions to communicate as if they were in the same region.

This topology is particularly useful for building geographically distributed and highly available architectures.

When designing Azure network topologies, it's essential to follow best practices for security.

Implement Network Security Groups (NSGs) to control inbound and outbound traffic to and from Azure resources.

NSGs allow you to define security rules that permit or deny traffic based on source and destination IP addresses, ports, and protocols.

By carefully configuring NSGs, you can enhance the security of your network and resources.

Additionally, consider using Azure Firewall to provide an additional layer of protection for your network.

Azure Firewall acts as a stateful firewall and can inspect and filter traffic at the application and network levels.

It's a scalable solution that helps safeguard your network from unauthorized access and threats.

To optimize network performance in Azure, consider using Azure Content Delivery Network (CDN) to deliver content to users with low-latency and high bandwidth.

CDN caches and replicates content in data centers around the world, reducing the load on your origin servers and improving user experience.

For even greater performance, you can leverage Azure ExpressRoute, a dedicated, high-speed connection to Azure's global network.

ExpressRoute offers predictable network performance, lower latency, and higher reliability compared to public internet connections.

It's an excellent choice for organizations with demanding network requirements.

When designing network topologies in Azure, it's also important to plan for network monitoring and diagnostics.

Azure Network Watcher provides a range of tools and capabilities to help you monitor, analyze, and troubleshoot your network.

Tools like Traffic Analytics, Connection Monitor, and Network Performance Monitor offer insights into network traffic patterns, connectivity issues, and performance bottlenecks.

By regularly monitoring your network, you can identify and resolve issues promptly, ensuring optimal network performance.

In terms of IP address management, consider using Azure IP Address Management (IPAM) to track and manage IP address assignments within your VNets.

IPAM helps you maintain accurate records of IP addresses, reducing the risk of IP conflicts and simplifying network management.

It's particularly useful in large or complex network environments.

When deploying Azure network topologies, keep in mind that network latency can impact application performance.

To mitigate latency, choose Azure regions that are geographically closer to your users and resources.

Azure offers a wide range of regions worldwide, allowing you to deploy resources in locations that optimize network proximity.

Additionally, use Azure Traffic Manager to implement global load balancing and route user requests to the nearest Azure region, further reducing latency and improving application responsiveness.

For organizations requiring high availability and disaster recovery, implement network redundancy and failover strategies.

Azure offers Azure Load Balancer to distribute incoming network traffic across multiple instances or VMs, ensuring high availability and fault tolerance.

Azure Traffic Manager can also play a role in disaster recovery by automatically redirecting traffic to healthy endpoints in the event of a failure.

Finally, consider implementing Azure Virtual Network peering across multiple regions to create redundant network paths and ensure continuity of operations.

In summary, Azure network topologies and best practices are essential for building secure, scalable, and high-performance cloud infrastructures.

Whether you're designing a hub-and-spoke network, VNet-to-VNet connections, or global network architectures, understanding the options and following security and performance best practices is critical.

By carefully planning and implementing your Azure network topology, you can create a resilient and efficient network environment that meets the needs of your organization's applications and workloads.

ExpressRoute and VPN connectivity are essential components of a robust and flexible network architecture in Azure.

These two options provide secure and reliable ways to connect your on-premises data centers and remote sites to Azure resources.

ExpressRoute is a dedicated, private network connection that extends your on-premises network into Azure.

It offers predictable performance, low latency, and high availability, making it an ideal choice for enterprises with stringent network requirements.

ExpressRoute connections are established through Microsoft's global network of partners, known as ExpressRoute providers, or by setting up a direct peering connection with Microsoft.

These connections bypass the public internet, ensuring a secure and reliable link between your on-premises infrastructure and Azure.

ExpressRoute offers multiple connection options, including private peering, public peering, and Microsoft peering, each serving different purposes and traffic types.

Private peering is used to connect to Azure private IP address space, enabling direct communication with resources within Azure VNets.

Public peering allows you to access Azure public services over ExpressRoute, such as Azure Storage and Azure SQL Database.

Microsoft peering is used to access Microsoft public services, such as Office 365, over ExpressRoute.

To set up ExpressRoute, you need to choose an ExpressRoute provider, select the appropriate peering options, and configure the routing for your on-premises network.

Once established, ExpressRoute connections can be used to access Azure resources and services as if they were part of your on-premises network.

Azure VPN Gateway, on the other hand, provides a secure and encrypted connection between your on-premises network and Azure through the public internet.

It's a versatile option suitable for smaller organizations or remote sites that don't require the dedicated connectivity of ExpressRoute.

Azure VPN Gateway supports several VPN protocols, including Site-to-Site VPN, Point-to-Site VPN, and VNet-to-VNet VPN, catering to various connectivity scenarios.

Site-to-Site VPN is used to create a secure connection between your on-premises network and an Azure VNet, extending your network into the cloud.

Point-to-Site VPN allows individual clients or devices to establish secure connections to Azure resources, offering remote access for users and devices.

VNet-to-VNet VPN enables secure communication between Azure VNets, useful for scenarios like multi-region deployments or connecting different Azure subscriptions.

When setting up Azure VPN Gateway, you need to configure the appropriate VPN type and protocols, create the necessary VPN connections, and define routing and security policies.

Azure VPN Gateway can be a cost-effective option for organizations looking to establish secure connections to Azure without the need for dedicated private circuits.

However, it's essential to consider the bandwidth and performance requirements of your network when choosing between ExpressRoute and VPN Gateway.

Both ExpressRoute and VPN Gateway offer high availability options, ensuring that your network connections remain resilient even in the face of hardware or software failures.

For ExpressRoute, you can set up redundant connections to two different ExpressRoute circuits, one primary and one secondary, to ensure continuous connectivity.

Azure VPN Gateway offers active-active and active-passive high availability configurations, depending on your specific needs.

In an active-active configuration, both VPN Gateways are active and share traffic load, while in an active-passive configuration, one VPN Gateway is active, and the other is on standby, ready to take over in case of a failure.

Monitoring and management of ExpressRoute and VPN Gateway connections are essential for maintaining network health and performance.

Azure provides monitoring tools such as Azure Network Watcher and Azure Monitor to help you gain insights into your network traffic, detect connectivity issues, and troubleshoot problems.

These tools allow you to capture and analyze network traffic, view connection status, and set up alerts for specific events.

Additionally, you can use Azure Traffic Manager to distribute incoming traffic across multiple VPN Gateway endpoints or ExpressRoute circuits, ensuring load balancing and fault tolerance.

When configuring ExpressRoute and VPN Gateway, consider implementing security measures to protect your network connections.

Both options support Network Security Groups (NSGs), which allow you to define inbound and outbound security rules to control traffic flow.

NSGs are a crucial component of network security in Azure and help protect your resources from unauthorized access and threats.

Additionally, Azure Firewall and Azure DDoS Protection provide advanced security features to safeguard your network and resources against cyberattacks.

In summary, ExpressRoute and VPN Gateway are essential connectivity options in Azure that enable secure and reliable communication between your on-premises network and Azure resources.

ExpressRoute offers dedicated, private connections with predictable performance, making it suitable for enterprises with stringent network requirements.

VPN Gateway, on the other hand, provides secure connections over the public internet, offering versatility and cost-effectiveness for various scenarios.

When choosing between the two options, consider your organization's bandwidth, performance, and security needs.

By carefully configuring and monitoring your network connections, you can ensure that your Azure infrastructure remains secure, reliable, and well-performing.

Chapter 4: Scalable Compute Solutions with Azure Virtual Machines

Selecting the right Azure VM types and sizing considerations are crucial steps in designing a cloud infrastructure that meets your application and workload requirements.

Azure offers a wide range of virtual machine (VM) types, each optimized for specific use cases and workloads.

Understanding your application's needs is essential when choosing the appropriate VM type.

Azure VM types are categorized based on their CPU, memory, and storage capacity, making it easier to match VMs to your requirements.

The first consideration when selecting VM types is CPU performance.

VMs are available in different CPU families, such as Intel and AMD, with varying numbers of vCPUs (virtual CPUs).

For compute-intensive workloads, VMs with higher CPU performance may be required to ensure optimal performance.

On the other hand, memory-intensive workloads benefit from VMs with a higher memory-to-vCPU ratio.

Azure provides a wide range of VM series, including General Purpose, Compute Optimized, Memory Optimized, and Storage Optimized, to address various performance needs.

General Purpose VMs offer a balance of CPU, memory, and storage resources, making them suitable for a wide range of applications, including web servers and development environments.

Compute Optimized VMs prioritize CPU performance and are ideal for scenarios like batch processing and scientific computing.

Memory Optimized VMs are designed for applications that require a large amount of memory, such as in-memory databases and analytics workloads.

Storage Optimized VMs are optimized for high-throughput storage and are suitable for applications that require fast access to large amounts of data.

Another important consideration when choosing VM types is storage performance.

Azure VMs come with different types of storage, including Standard HDD, Standard SSD, Premium SSD, and Ultra Disk, each offering different levels of performance and durability.

Standard HDD provides cost-effective storage with moderate performance and is suitable for less demanding workloads.

Standard SSD offers a balance of cost and performance and is a good choice for general-purpose applications.

Premium SSD delivers high-performance storage with low latency and is recommended for mission-critical applications and databases.

Ultra Disk provides the highest level of performance and is ideal for applications that demand the fastest storage access.

When sizing VMs, it's essential to consider the number of vCPUs and the amount of memory required by your applications.

Azure VM sizes range from small instances with a few vCPUs and limited memory to large instances with multiple vCPUs and large memory capacities.

To determine the appropriate VM size, you can use Azure's VM sizing tools and guidelines, which help you estimate CPU and memory requirements based on your application's workload characteristics.

Consider workload peaks and fluctuations when sizing VMs to ensure that your infrastructure can handle variations in demand.

Azure offers VMs that support auto-scaling, allowing you to automatically adjust the number of VM instances based on workload changes.

This feature helps optimize resource utilization and cost efficiency.

In addition to CPU, memory, and storage considerations, it's essential to factor in network bandwidth and latency requirements when selecting VM types.

Azure provides VMs with varying levels of network performance, and you should choose VMs that align with your network needs.

Azure also offers VMs with accelerated networking capabilities, which can significantly improve network performance for applications that require low-latency communication.

When selecting VM types, you should also consider licensing and software requirements.

Azure provides various licensing options, including pay-as-you-go, reserved instances, and bring-your-own-license (BYOL) models.

Evaluate your licensing needs to determine the most cost-effective option for your organization.

Additionally, consider the availability and redundancy requirements of your applications.

Azure offers Virtual Machine Scale Sets (VMSS), which allow you to deploy and manage a group of identical VMs.

VMSS can provide high availability and load balancing for your applications by distributing traffic across multiple instances.

When planning for redundancy and availability, you should also consider Azure Availability Zones, which provide data center-level redundancy and fault tolerance.

Azure's global presence and data center regions allow you to deploy VMs in multiple geographic locations for disaster recovery and business continuity purposes.

Finally, budget constraints and cost optimization are critical factors when selecting VM types.

Azure offers various pricing options, including on-demand, reserved, and spot instances.

By carefully evaluating your workload requirements and usage patterns, you can optimize your VM selection to minimize costs while meeting performance and availability objectives.

In summary, choosing the right Azure VM types and sizing considerations is essential for designing a cloud infrastructure that meets your application and workload needs.

Consider factors such as CPU performance, memory, storage, and network requirements when selecting VM types.

Use Azure's VM sizing tools and guidelines to estimate CPU and memory requirements accurately.

Factor in network performance, licensing, redundancy, and budget constraints to make informed decisions that align with your organization's goals.

By carefully selecting and sizing Azure VMs, you can create a cost-effective and high-performing cloud infrastructure that supports your applications and workloads effectively.

Load balancing and auto-scaling are essential techniques for ensuring the availability, performance, and reliability of virtual machines (VMs) in a cloud infrastructure.

Load balancing helps distribute incoming network traffic evenly across multiple VM instances, ensuring that no single instance becomes overwhelmed and leading to improved application responsiveness and fault tolerance.

Azure offers Azure Load Balancer, a cloud-based load balancer service that can distribute traffic across multiple VMs within a virtual network (VNet).

Azure Load Balancer operates at both the transport layer (Layer 4) and the application layer (Layer 7), providing flexibility in load balancing scenarios.

Load balancing can be configured for various types of workloads, including web applications, APIs, and database servers.

To set up load balancing, you define a backend pool of VMs that will receive traffic, configure load balancing rules to specify how traffic should be distributed, and define health probes to monitor the health of VM instances.

Azure Load Balancer supports both inbound and outbound traffic, making it suitable for a wide range of scenarios.

In addition to distributing traffic, load balancing can also help improve the availability of your applications.

Azure Load Balancer offers high availability configurations by allowing you to distribute traffic across VM instances deployed in different availability zones or availability sets.

This redundancy ensures that your applications remain accessible even if a VM instance or an entire zone becomes unavailable due to hardware failures or maintenance.

Auto-scaling, on the other hand, allows you to automatically adjust the number of VM instances based on workload demands.

Azure provides two auto-scaling solutions: Azure Virtual Machine Scale Sets (VMSS) and Azure Autoscale.

VMSS allows you to deploy and manage a group of identical VMs, and it provides built-in auto-scaling capabilities.

With VMSS, you can define scaling rules that specify conditions for scaling in and out, such as CPU utilization or memory consumption.

When a rule's conditions are met, VMSS automatically adds or removes VM instances to maintain the desired capacity.

Azure Autoscale, on the other hand, is a service that can be used to auto-scale individual VMs or other Azure resources, such as Azure App Service instances or Azure Functions.

Autoscale uses metric-based rules to determine when to scale resources and allows you to configure thresholds and scaling actions.

For example, you can set up an autoscale rule to add additional VM instances when CPU utilization exceeds a certain threshold and remove them when the load decreases.

By combining load balancing and auto-scaling, you can create a highly available and elastic architecture that can handle fluctuations in traffic and workload demands.

For example, during periods of high traffic, load balancing can evenly distribute incoming requests across multiple VM instances, preventing any single instance from becoming a bottleneck.

If the traffic continues to increase, auto-scaling can dynamically add more VM instances to handle the load, ensuring that your application remains responsive and available.

Conversely, during periods of low traffic, auto-scaling can remove unnecessary VM instances, saving on operational costs.

Azure provides integration between load balancing and auto-scaling services to create seamless and dynamic scaling solutions.

For instance, you can configure Azure Load Balancer to distribute traffic to VM instances in a VMSS.

When the VMSS scales out by adding new instances, the load balancer automatically includes them in the pool, ensuring that the new instances receive traffic.

Likewise, when VM instances are removed during scale-in, the load balancer automatically adjusts to distribute traffic among the remaining instances.

Additionally, you can use Azure Application Gateway, another load balancing service with web application firewall (WAF) capabilities, to provide advanced load balancing and application delivery features for web applications.

Application Gateway offers features such as URL-based routing, SSL offloading, and cookie-based session affinity, making it suitable for complex application scenarios.

In summary, load balancing and auto-scaling are critical components of a cloud infrastructure strategy to ensure application availability, performance, and cost efficiency.

Azure offers load balancing services like Azure Load Balancer and Azure Application Gateway to distribute incoming traffic across VM instances and provide high availability.

Azure also provides auto-scaling solutions such as Azure Virtual Machine Scale Sets (VMSS) and Azure Autoscale to dynamically adjust the number of VM instances based on workload demands.

By combining load balancing and auto-scaling, organizations can create resilient and elastic architectures that respond to changing traffic patterns and workload requirements, ultimately delivering a better user experience and optimizing resource utilization.

Chapter 5: Storage and Data Management Strategies

Azure Storage Services are a fundamental component of Microsoft Azure, providing a scalable and reliable way to store, manage, and access data in the cloud.

Azure offers a variety of storage services designed to accommodate different data types, workloads, and accessibility requirements.

One of the core storage services in Azure is Azure Blob Storage, which is optimized for storing unstructured data, such as documents, images, videos, and backups.

Azure Blob Storage provides highly durable and available storage, making it suitable for a wide range of use cases, from media streaming to data backup.

Another key storage service is Azure Files, which offers fully managed file shares in the cloud, accessible through the Server Message Block (SMB) protocol.

Azure Files is a great choice for migrating file-based applications to the cloud, sharing files across multiple VMs, and providing remote access to shared data.

For structured data, Azure Table Storage provides a NoSQL data store that is highly scalable and cost-effective.

It's designed for scenarios where fast and flexible querying of semi-structured data is required, making it suitable for applications like IoT telemetry, user profiles, and metadata storage.

Azure Queue Storage, on the other hand, is a messaging service that allows decoupled communication between application components, helping to build resilient and scalable cloud applications.

Applications can use Azure Queue Storage to pass messages asynchronously, ensuring loose coupling and fault tolerance.

Azure also offers premium storage options, such as Azure Premium Blob Storage and Azure Premium File Storage, which provide higher levels of performance and lower latency for demanding workloads.

These premium storage offerings are ideal for scenarios like big data analytics, artificial intelligence, and high-performance computing.

For disk storage associated with Azure Virtual Machines, Azure Managed Disks simplify the management and scaling of virtual hard disks (VHDs).

Managed Disks come in different performance tiers, including Standard HDD, Standard SSD, Premium SSD, and Ultra Disk, allowing you to choose the right disk type for your VMs and workloads.

Azure Storage Services are highly available and durable, with data replicated across multiple data centers to protect against hardware failures and data loss.

Data in Azure Storage is also encrypted at rest and in transit, ensuring the security and privacy of your data.

Azure provides redundancy options, including locally redundant storage (LRS), geo-redundant storage (GRS), and zone-redundant storage (ZRS), to meet various data residency and disaster recovery requirements.

Azure Storage is accessible through a REST API, SDKs for various programming languages, and Azure Portal, providing flexibility for developers and administrators to interact with and manage their data.

Azure also offers data transfer solutions, such as Azure Data Box and Azure Data Box Disk, to help you securely move large volumes of data to and from Azure.

For hybrid cloud scenarios, Azure offers Azure File Sync, a service that synchronizes on-premises file servers with Azure Files, providing a centralized and cloud-backed file share.

Azure Storage Services integrate seamlessly with other Azure services, allowing you to build powerful and scalable cloud applications.

For example, Azure Blob Storage can be used as a backend for web applications, and Azure Functions can trigger actions based on changes to data in Azure Storage.

Azure Data Factory enables data integration and transformation workflows with Azure Storage as a data source or destination.

Furthermore, Azure Storage supports data analytics and machine learning workloads through services like Azure Data Lake Storage and Azure Databricks.

Azure Data Lake Storage is optimized for big data analytics and provides features like hierarchical namespace and fine-grained access control.

Azure Databricks, a big data analytics platform, can directly access data stored in Azure Storage, making it easier to build and train machine learning models at scale.

In summary, Azure Storage Services offer a comprehensive and flexible storage solution for organizations of all sizes.

Whether you need to store unstructured data, structured data, files, or messages, Azure provides a range of storage services to meet your needs.

With high availability, durability, and security features, Azure Storage Services are a reliable choice for building and deploying cloud-native applications and services.

Their seamless integration with other Azure services enables you to leverage the full power of the Azure cloud platform to innovate and deliver value to your organization.

Data backup and recovery are critical aspects of any organization's data management strategy, and Microsoft Azure offers a robust set of solutions to help protect your data in the cloud.

Azure Backup is a fully managed service that allows you to back up and restore data for virtual machines, on-premises servers, and Azure File Shares.

With Azure Backup, you can protect your data against accidental deletions, hardware failures, and other data loss scenarios.

Azure Backup also supports long-term retention, enabling you to store data for extended periods, ensuring compliance with data retention policies and regulations.

Azure Site Recovery is another essential service that provides disaster recovery and business continuity solutions.

It allows you to replicate on-premises workloads and virtual machines to Azure, ensuring that your applications remain available in case of a site-wide outage or disaster.

Azure Site Recovery provides failover and failback capabilities, helping you minimize downtime and data loss during recovery operations.

For applications that require continuous data replication, Azure offers Azure SQL Database Geo-Replication.

This service allows you to replicate your SQL databases to different Azure regions, providing a high level of data availability and resilience against regional outages.

You can configure geo-replication for read-only access or as a failover option for disaster recovery.

Azure Blob Storage also offers built-in data protection features, such as soft delete and versioning.

Soft delete allows you to recover data that was accidentally deleted or modified within a specified retention period, providing an added layer of protection against data loss.

Versioning enables you to preserve and access previous versions of your data, which can be valuable for compliance and auditing purposes.

In addition to these data protection services, Azure offers Azure File Sync, a solution that enables synchronization between on-premises file servers and Azure File Shares.

Azure File Sync helps organizations centralize and protect their file data in Azure while providing fast and efficient access to data from remote offices or branch locations.

Another important aspect of data backup and recovery is monitoring and reporting.

Azure provides comprehensive monitoring and reporting capabilities through Azure Monitor and Azure Security Center.

Azure Monitor allows you to track the performance and availability of your resources and set up alerting for data protection-related events, such as backup failures or storage capacity issues.

Azure Security Center offers security recommendations and threat detection to help you identify and mitigate potential risks to your data.

It also provides insights into your data protection posture and compliance with industry standards and regulations.

When it comes to data recovery, Azure provides several options for restoring your data.

Azure Backup allows you to restore individual files and folders, full virtual machines, or even entire on-premises servers to a specific point in time.

You can choose to recover data to the original location or an alternate location, depending on your recovery needs.

Azure Site Recovery offers automated failover and failback capabilities for virtual machines, ensuring a smooth recovery process in case of a disaster.

Azure SQL Database Geo-Replication enables you to fail over to a secondary region in the event of a regional outage, minimizing downtime and data loss.

Azure Blob Storage's soft delete and versioning features allow you to recover deleted data or access previous versions of your blobs when needed.

Azure File Sync provides a self-service restore option for end-users, allowing them to recover files and folders from the synchronized file share.

In summary, data backup and recovery solutions in Azure are designed to protect your data and ensure its availability in various scenarios, from accidental deletions to site-wide disasters.

Azure Backup, Azure Site Recovery, Azure SQL Database Geo-Replication, and Azure File Sync offer a range of options for data protection and disaster recovery.

Azure also provides monitoring and reporting capabilities through Azure Monitor and Azure Security Center to help you proactively manage and secure your data.

With Azure's comprehensive data protection and recovery solutions, you can confidently build and operate resilient and reliable cloud-based applications and services.

Chapter 6: Advanced Azure Security and Compliance

Azure Security Center is a comprehensive security management and threat protection service provided by Microsoft Azure.

It serves as a central hub for monitoring and enhancing the security of your Azure resources and hybrid workloads.

Azure Security Center provides a unified view of your security posture across your Azure subscriptions, helping you identify and address security vulnerabilities and threats.

One of the key features of Azure Security Center is its threat detection capability, which continuously analyzes telemetry data from your Azure resources to detect and alert you about potential security threats.

Azure Security Center employs advanced analytics and machine learning to identify suspicious activities and potential security incidents.

It can detect a wide range of threats, including malware infections, suspicious login attempts, unauthorized access, and unusual data access patterns.

When a potential threat is detected, Azure Security Center generates alerts and provides detailed information about the suspicious activity.

These alerts are categorized by severity, helping you prioritize and respond to security incidents effectively.

Azure Security Center also offers recommendations and best practices to help you remediate security vulnerabilities and reduce the attack surface of your Azure resources.

It provides security policies and compliance assessments based on industry standards and regulatory requirements, such as CIS (Center for Internet Security) benchmarks and GDPR (General Data Protection Regulation).

Azure Security Center can automatically assess the security configuration of your resources and provide remediation steps to address any misconfigurations.

Furthermore, it offers just-in-time (JIT) access control, which allows you to restrict access to your virtual machines by temporarily opening network ports only when needed.

This minimizes the exposure of your resources to potential attacks.

Azure Security Center also integrates with Azure Active Directory Identity Protection to provide additional threat detection capabilities for your identity and access management.

It can detect suspicious user activities and risky sign-ins, helping you protect your organization's identities.

Azure Security Center provides threat intelligence feeds and threat indicators, allowing you to stay informed about emerging threats and vulnerabilities.

It can automatically correlate threat data with your Azure resources, helping you prioritize security incidents and take appropriate action.

For organizations with advanced security needs, Azure Security Center offers integration with Azure Sentinel, Microsoft's cloud-native security information and event management (SIEM) solution.

This integration enables you to collect, analyze, and act on security data from various sources, including Azure Security Center alerts.

Azure Security Center also supports threat hunting, allowing security analysts to proactively search for and investigate potential security threats.

It provides a query language and customizable queries to help analysts uncover hidden threats and vulnerabilities.

To enhance the security of your Azure virtual machines, Azure Security Center offers just-in-time (JIT) VM access.

This feature allows you to restrict inbound traffic to your virtual machines and open network ports only when necessary.

JIT VM access reduces the attack surface and helps protect your virtual machines from unauthorized access.

Azure Security Center also provides endpoint protection recommendations, helping you ensure that your virtual machines are running up-to-date anti-malware software.

Additionally, it offers advanced threat protection for Azure SQL Database, helping you detect and respond to potential threats targeting your database.

In summary, Azure Security Center is a powerful security management and threat protection service that helps you safeguard your Azure resources and hybrid workloads.

It provides continuous threat detection, security recommendations, and compliance assessments to enhance your security posture.

Azure Security Center integrates with other Azure services and offers advanced features like just-in-time access control, threat hunting, and integration with Azure Sentinel.

By leveraging Azure Security Center, you can strengthen the security of your Azure environment and protect your organization from evolving cyber threats.

Compliance is a critical consideration for organizations when it comes to adopting cloud services like Microsoft Azure.

It involves adhering to industry-specific regulations, standards, and best practices to ensure that data and systems are secure and meet legal requirements.

Azure provides a robust set of tools and features to help organizations achieve and maintain compliance with various frameworks and auditing requirements.

One of the primary compliance frameworks addressed by Azure is the General Data Protection Regulation (GDPR), which is crucial for organizations handling personal data of European Union (EU) citizens.

Azure offers a comprehensive set of services and features to help customers comply with GDPR, including data encryption, access controls, and tools for data protection impact assessments.

Additionally, Azure has implemented strict security measures, such as role-based access control (RBAC) and multi-factor authentication (MFA), to safeguard sensitive data.

Azure also offers a Data Subject Request (DSR) capability, allowing organizations to respond to data subject access requests in compliance with GDPR.

For organizations in the healthcare sector, Azure adheres to the Health Insurance Portability and Accountability Act (HIPAA) requirements.

Azure provides a HIPAA Business Associate Agreement (BAA) for eligible customers, ensuring that Azure services can be used for protected health information (PHI) in a compliant manner.

Azure's security and compliance capabilities are designed to meet the stringent requirements of HIPAA, such as data encryption, auditing, and access controls.

Another critical compliance framework addressed by Azure is the Payment Card Industry Data Security Standard (PCI DSS), which is essential for organizations handling credit card payments.

Azure offers a PCI DSS compliance package that includes a PCI Attestation of Compliance (AoC) and a Responsibility Matrix.

This package helps customers understand their responsibilities in achieving PCI DSS compliance while using Azure services.

Azure provides secure networking options, like Azure Virtual Network, to segregate and protect cardholder data environments.

Moreover, Azure offers a secure payment card industry (PCI) blueprint that simplifies the process of building a PCI-compliant architecture in the cloud.

For organizations in the government and public sector, Azure Government is a dedicated cloud environment that adheres to strict compliance standards, including FedRAMP, CJIS, and ITAR.

Azure Government provides a secure and compliant platform for government agencies, law enforcement organizations, and organizations with federal compliance requirements.

Azure Government also offers Azure Policy and Azure Blueprints to help organizations enforce compliance with specific regulatory requirements and internal policies.

In addition to industry-specific compliance frameworks, Azure also supports regional and international standards, such as ISO 27001, SOC 1, SOC 2, and NIST.

Azure undergoes regular third-party audits to validate its compliance with these standards and provides audit reports and certifications to customers.

Azure's compliance documentation and resources, such as the Microsoft Compliance Manager and Azure Security and Compliance Blueprint, assist organizations in assessing their compliance posture and addressing any compliance gaps.

Azure Policy is a key tool for enforcing compliance within an organization's Azure environment.

It allows administrators to define and enforce policies to ensure that resources deployed in Azure adhere to specific compliance standards and requirements.

Azure Policy helps prevent non-compliant resource deployments and provides continuous monitoring and reporting on compliance status.

Furthermore, Azure offers a wide range of auditing and monitoring capabilities to help organizations track and analyze activities in their Azure environments.

Azure Monitor provides comprehensive insights into the performance and health of Azure resources and services.

Azure Security Center offers advanced threat detection and monitoring to identify security threats and vulnerabilities.

Azure Activity Log records all activities performed on Azure resources, allowing organizations to review and audit changes made to their environment.

Azure Monitor Logs enable the collection and analysis of log data from Azure services, custom applications, and on-premises resources.

Organizations can use Azure Monitor Logs for security information and event management (SIEM), threat detection, and compliance reporting.

Azure's compliance framework and auditing capabilities provide organizations with the tools and resources they need to achieve and maintain compliance with various regulatory standards and industry-specific requirements.

Whether it's GDPR, HIPAA, PCI DSS, or other compliance frameworks, Azure offers a secure and compliant cloud platform to help organizations protect sensitive data and meet their compliance obligations.

By leveraging Azure's built-in security controls, compliance resources, and auditing features, organizations can confidently adopt cloud services while ensuring the security and compliance of their workloads and data.

Chapter 7: Orchestrating Workloads with Azure Automation

Azure Automation is a powerful cloud-based service that allows organizations to automate tasks, configure systems, and manage resources in a consistent and efficient manner.

One of the key components of Azure Automation is Desired State Configuration (DSC), which is a management platform that enables organizations to define and maintain the desired state of their systems.

DSC allows administrators to declare what the configuration of a system should be and then ensure that the system remains in that desired state.

With Azure Automation DSC, organizations can automate the configuration and management of both Windows and Linux systems, ensuring consistency and reducing manual administrative efforts.

One of the primary benefits of Azure Automation DSC is its ability to define configurations as code, which means that administrators can specify the configuration settings for their systems using a declarative syntax.

This approach makes it easier to define, manage, and version the configurations for various systems, reducing the risk of configuration drift and errors.

Azure Automation DSC provides a central repository, known as the Azure Automation State Configuration (AA DSC) service, where administrators can store and manage their configuration scripts and modules.

These configuration scripts and modules can be reused across multiple systems, making it efficient to maintain a consistent configuration across the organization's infrastructure.

To apply a configuration to a target system, administrators can create and assign a DSC configuration to the system using Azure Automation.

Once assigned, Azure Automation DSC will automatically monitor and enforce the desired state of the system, ensuring that it complies with the defined configuration settings.

Azure Automation DSC can also generate reports and provide insights into the compliance status of systems, allowing administrators to track and remediate any configuration deviations.

Another key feature of Azure Automation DSC is its support for both push and pull modes of configuration enforcement.

In push mode, administrators can initiate configuration updates and enforce the desired state on target systems directly from the Azure Automation portal or through automation scripts.

In pull mode, target systems regularly check for configuration updates in the Azure Automation State Configuration service and apply them as needed.

This pull-based approach is particularly useful for managing large and distributed environments where administrators want to minimize the need for direct communication with target systems.

Azure Automation DSC supports a wide range of configuration scenarios, including server roles, features, software installations, registry settings, and file configurations.

Administrators can also use DSC to manage configurations for various applications and services running on their systems.

Furthermore, Azure Automation DSC integrates with other Azure services and capabilities, such as Azure Resource Manager templates, Azure DevOps, and Azure Monitor.

This integration enables organizations to incorporate DSC into their infrastructure as code (IaC) and continuous integration/continuous deployment (CI/CD) pipelines.

With Azure Resource Manager templates, administrators can define and deploy entire Azure environments, including DSC configurations, in a repeatable and automated manner.

Azure DevOps pipelines can be used to automate the testing and deployment of DSC configurations as part of the application deployment process.

Azure Monitor can provide insights into the health and compliance of systems managed by Azure Automation DSC, helping organizations proactively detect and address configuration issues.

In summary, Azure Automation and Desired State Configuration (DSC) provide organizations with a powerful platform for automating and managing the configuration of their systems and resources in a consistent and efficient manner.

DSC allows administrators to define configurations as code, ensuring that systems remain in their desired state and reducing the risk of configuration drift.

Azure Automation DSC supports push and pull modes of configuration enforcement, making it flexible and scalable for managing various scenarios.

Integrations with other Azure services and capabilities enable organizations to incorporate DSC into their infrastructure as code and CI/CD pipelines, streamlining the deployment and management of their environments.

By leveraging Azure Automation DSC, organizations can achieve greater consistency, efficiency, and control in their configuration management processes, ultimately enhancing the reliability and security of their systems.

Creating and managing runbooks is a fundamental aspect of

Azure Automation, allowing organizations to automate various tasks, processes, and workflows in their Azure environments.

A runbook is a collection of one or more automation scripts and activities that can be executed manually or on a schedule to perform specific actions or operations.

Azure Automation provides a centralized and scalable platform for designing, authoring, and orchestrating runbooks to streamline operational tasks and improve efficiency.

Runbooks in Azure Automation can be categorized into two main types: graphical and textual.

Graphical runbooks are created using the Azure portal's graphical editor, allowing users to design automation processes visually by arranging activities in a flowchart-like manner.

Textual runbooks, on the other hand, are authored using Windows PowerShell Workflow (PSWorkflow) or Python scripting languages, providing greater flexibility and control for complex automation scenarios.

To create a graphical runbook, users can navigate to the Azure Automation account in the Azure portal and use the graphical editor to design the runbook's workflow.

Activities such as starting and stopping virtual machines, sending email notifications, or running custom scripts can be added to the runbook's design canvas and connected in a sequence to define the automation logic.

Each activity in the graphical runbook corresponds to a specific action or operation, and users can configure input parameters, output variables, and error handling for each activity.

Once the graphical runbook is designed, it can be published and made available for execution within Azure Automation.

Textual runbooks, on the other hand, are created using PowerShell Workflow or Python scripts, providing more advanced scripting capabilities for automation tasks.

Users can author these runbooks in the Azure portal's code editor or develop them locally using their preferred Integrated Development Environment (IDE) and then import them into Azure Automation.

Textual runbooks can include logic, conditions, loops, and external modules, making them suitable for a wide range of automation scenarios.

Azure Automation offers a library of pre-built runbook modules and script samples that users can leverage to streamline the creation of their automation runbooks.

Once created, runbooks can be associated with schedules, allowing them to run automatically at specified times or intervals.

Users can configure schedules based on their organization's operational requirements, ensuring that routine tasks are performed consistently and without manual intervention.

Additionally, runbooks can be executed manually whenever needed, providing flexibility for ad-hoc tasks or troubleshooting scenarios.

Azure Automation also offers capabilities for monitoring and logging runbook executions.

Users can view the runbook job status, review execution logs, and access detailed reports to track the outcome and performance of their automation tasks.

Logging and reporting help organizations maintain visibility and accountability for their automated processes.

Moreover, runbooks in Azure Automation can take advantage of assets such as variables, credentials, and connections.

Variables allow users to store and reuse values across runbooks, making it easier to manage configuration settings and input parameters.

Credentials enable secure access to resources and systems by storing login information securely within Azure Automation.

Connections provide reusable endpoint configurations for connecting to external systems, databases, or cloud services.

These assets enhance the reusability and security of runbooks while simplifying the management of sensitive information.

Azure Automation also supports the concept of hybrid runbooks, which can be executed both in Azure and on-premises environments.

This capability is valuable for organizations with hybrid infrastructures, as it allows automation to span across cloud and on-premises resources seamlessly.

To facilitate the creation and management of runbooks, Azure Automation provides source control integration, allowing users to link their Azure Automation account to a source control repository such as Azure DevOps or GitHub.

This integration enables version control, collaboration, and change tracking for runbooks, ensuring that automation scripts are maintained and updated efficiently.

Azure Automation also supports runbook testing, enabling users to validate their automation logic and scripts in a safe and controlled environment before deploying them in production.

Testing helps identify and resolve potential issues or errors in runbooks, reducing the risk of unintended consequences during execution.

In summary, creating and managing runbooks in Azure Automation is a fundamental practice for automating operational tasks and processes in Azure environments.

Users can choose between graphical and textual runbooks to design automation workflows, schedule them for automatic execution, and monitor their performance.

Assets like variables, credentials, and connections enhance the reusability and security of runbooks, while source control integration and testing capabilities support efficient runbook development and maintenance.

By leveraging Azure Automation's runbook capabilities, organizations can achieve greater operational efficiency, reduce manual efforts, and ensure consistent and reliable execution of their automation tasks.

Chapter 8: Enterprise Application Deployment and Integration

Azure App Services provide a powerful platform for building, deploying, and managing web and mobile applications in the cloud.

These services simplify application development by handling infrastructure management, scaling, and monitoring, allowing developers to focus on writing code and delivering value to their users.

Azure App Services offer various deployment options and hosting plans, catering to a wide range of application scenarios and requirements.

One of the core deployment options for Azure App Services is Web Apps, which allow developers to host web applications built using various programming languages and frameworks, including .NET, Java, Node.js, Python, and PHP.

Web Apps provide a scalable and fully managed hosting environment with built-in load balancing, auto-scaling, and high availability.

Developers can deploy their web applications directly from their preferred Integrated Development Environment (IDE), source control repository, or continuous integration/continuous deployment (CI/CD) pipeline.

Azure also offers Mobile Apps, a specialized type of App Service designed for hosting mobile app backends and APIs.

Mobile Apps support cross-platform development and provide features like authentication, offline data sync, and push notifications to simplify mobile app development.

Additionally, API Apps are designed to host RESTful APIs and microservices, making it easy to expose and manage APIs in a scalable and secure manner.

Azure Functions, another deployment option, is a serverless compute service that allows developers to write and deploy event-driven functions without worrying about server infrastructure.

Functions can be triggered by various Azure services, such as Azure Blob Storage, Azure Queue Storage, or Azure Event Hubs, as well as external events like HTTP requests.

These functions can be written in multiple programming languages, including C#, JavaScript, Python, and PowerShell.

Docker Containers offer another powerful deployment option within Azure App Services, allowing developers to package their applications and dependencies into containers and run them on a container-based hosting platform.

This approach provides application portability and flexibility, making it easy to deploy applications consistently across different environments.

Azure App Services also offer a choice of hosting plans, each tailored to specific workload requirements.

The Shared hosting plan is a cost-effective option for hosting small-scale web applications with shared resources.

It is suitable for development and testing scenarios with low traffic or resource demands.

The Basic hosting plan provides dedicated resources for web applications, ensuring consistent performance and isolated application environments.

It is suitable for production workloads with moderate traffic and resource requirements.

The Standard hosting plan offers additional features like automatic scaling, custom domains, and backup capabilities.

It is ideal for production applications with higher traffic and resource demands.

The Premium hosting plan offers enhanced performance, security, and scale-out capabilities, making it suitable for mission-critical applications with high availability and resource requirements.

Azure also provides the App Service Environment (ASE), which is a premium service plan offering a fully isolated and highly secure environment for hosting applications.

ASE is designed for applications that require strict network isolation, compliance with regulatory standards, and high availability.

Additionally, developers can choose between Windows-based and Linux-based hosting environments for their Azure App Services.

Azure App Services support both Windows and Linux operating systems, allowing developers to select the platform that best fits their application's requirements and technology stack.

The Azure portal provides a user-friendly interface for managing Azure App Services, enabling developers to deploy, monitor, scale, and configure their applications with ease.

It offers features like deployment slots, which allow developers to create staging environments for testing and validation before promoting changes to production.

Deployment slots help minimize downtime and ensure a smooth deployment process.

Azure also provides integration with popular development tools, such as Visual Studio, Visual Studio Code, and Azure DevOps, to streamline application development and deployment workflows.

Moreover, Azure offers extensive support for DevOps practices by enabling continuous integration and continuous deployment (CI/CD) pipelines.

Developers can leverage Azure DevOps Services or other CI/CD tools to automate the build, test, and deployment processes for their Azure App Services.

By implementing CI/CD pipelines, teams can achieve faster and more reliable application delivery while maintaining code quality and consistency.

Furthermore, Azure App Services offer robust monitoring and diagnostics capabilities to help developers gain insights into the performance and health of their applications.

Azure Application Insights, integrated with Azure App Services, provides real-time telemetry data, performance metrics, and error tracking.

Developers can use this data to identify and troubleshoot issues, optimize application performance, and gain valuable insights into user behavior.

In summary, Azure App Services provide a versatile and powerful platform for hosting web and mobile applications in the cloud.

With a variety of deployment options, hosting plans, and support for both Windows and Linux environments, Azure App Services cater to a wide range of application scenarios and requirements.

Developers can leverage Azure's robust set of tools, integrations, and DevOps practices to streamline application development, deployment, and monitoring processes, ultimately delivering high-quality applications to their users.

Azure Integration Services offer a comprehensive suite of tools and services designed to help enterprises connect, integrate, and orchestrate their applications and data across the cloud and on-premises environments.

These services provide the necessary building blocks for building scalable and reliable integration solutions to meet the complex needs of modern enterprises.

One of the key components of Azure Integration Services is Azure Logic Apps, which enables organizations to create and run workflows that integrate with various services, systems, and applications.

Logic Apps use a visual designer that allows users to define workflows by connecting pre-built connectors and triggers, making it easy to automate business processes and data flows.

Azure Logic Apps support a wide range of connectors, including popular SaaS applications, on-premises systems, and Azure services, allowing organizations to create seamless integrations across their entire ecosystem.

Another critical element of Azure Integration Services is Azure Service Bus, which provides a messaging platform for building scalable and decoupled applications.

Service Bus supports both message-based and event-driven communication patterns, making it suitable for scenarios like application integration, event sourcing, and IoT telemetry.

Organizations can use Azure Service Bus to ensure reliable message delivery, publish-subscribe messaging, and message routing across their distributed applications.

Azure API Management is another essential service within the integration suite, allowing enterprises to publish, secure, and manage APIs for their applications.

API Management offers features like rate limiting, authentication, and analytics, empowering organizations to expose and monetize their APIs while maintaining control and security.

Azure Functions, part of the serverless compute offerings, can be leveraged for building event-driven and microservices-based integrations.

Developers can write serverless functions that execute in response to events, such as HTTP requests, queue messages, or timer triggers, enabling them to implement lightweight and scalable integration logic.

Azure Event Grid extends event-driven integration capabilities by providing a managed event routing service that simplifies the creation of event-driven architectures.

Event Grid supports events from various Azure services, custom events, and external sources, allowing organizations to react to events in real-time and trigger automated workflows.

Azure Data Factory is a data integration service that enables enterprises to create, schedule, and manage data-driven workflows for ETL (Extract, Transform, Load) and data integration scenarios.

Data Factory supports hybrid data integration, allowing organizations to move data between on-premises and cloud environments seamlessly.

Azure Integration Services also offer Azure Data Share, a service that facilitates secure data sharing between organizations or departments by providing fine-grained control over data access and sharing policies.

Data Share is particularly valuable for enterprises looking to collaborate on data-driven initiatives while maintaining data privacy and compliance.

Azure Integration Services include Azure Logic Apps Enterprise Integration Pack, which enhances Logic Apps' capabilities by providing B2B (business-to-business) and EDI (Electronic Data Interchange) capabilities.

This pack enables organizations to exchange business documents and messages with their partners in various standard formats, making it suitable for supply chain and trading partner integration scenarios.

Azure Integration Services can be easily extended with Azure Functions to implement custom logic for processing, transforming, and enriching data as it flows through integration workflows.

By combining Logic Apps, Azure Functions, and other integration services, organizations can build robust and flexible integration solutions tailored to their specific requirements.

Azure Integration Services also integrate seamlessly with Azure DevOps, enabling organizations to adopt a DevOps approach to manage the development, testing, deployment, and monitoring of their integration solutions.

This integration ensures that integration solutions can be developed and maintained using the same best practices and processes as the rest of the application portfolio.

Moreover, Azure Integration Services support monitoring, tracking, and auditing of integration workflows to ensure visibility into their performance and reliability.

Organizations can use Azure Monitor, Azure Application Insights, and Azure Log Analytics to gain insights into the health and behavior of their integrations.

These services provide rich telemetry data, dashboards, and alerts to help organizations identify and resolve issues quickly.

In summary, Azure Integration Services offer a comprehensive set of tools and services that empower enterprises to connect, integrate, and orchestrate their applications and data seamlessly.

From Logic Apps for workflow automation to Service Bus for messaging and API Management for API governance, these services provide the building blocks for building robust and scalable integration solutions.

Whether it's connecting on-premises systems, creating event-driven architectures, or facilitating data sharing, Azure Integration Services enable organizations to meet the complex integration needs of modern enterprises while embracing best practices in DevOps, monitoring, and security.

Chapter 9: Optimizing Cost and Resource Management in Azure

Cost control and budgeting are critical aspects of managing your resources effectively in Azure.

With its flexible and scalable cloud services, Azure provides the tools and capabilities you need to optimize your spending and ensure that your cloud investments align with your business objectives.

To achieve effective cost control in Azure, it's essential to start with a clear understanding of your organization's goals and priorities.

By defining your business objectives and mapping them to your cloud strategy, you can make informed decisions about which Azure services to use and how to allocate your resources effectively.

One of the key principles of cost control in Azure is the concept of "pay as you go."

Azure offers a consumption-based pricing model, meaning you only pay for the resources you actually use.

This allows you to avoid upfront capital expenses and scale your resources up or down as needed, based on demand.

To gain visibility into your Azure spending, you can use Azure Cost Management and Billing, a powerful tool that provides insights into your usage and spending patterns.

Azure Cost Management and Billing offer detailed reports and dashboards that allow you to track your spending, identify cost trends, and understand how different Azure services contribute to your overall expenses.

With this information, you can make informed decisions about resource allocation and optimization.

Another essential aspect of cost control is setting up budgets and alerts.

Azure allows you to create budgets that define spending thresholds for specific Azure subscriptions or resource groups.

You can set up alerts to notify you when your spending exceeds predefined limits, helping you proactively manage your costs.

Budgets and alerts ensure that you have real-time visibility into your spending and can take immediate action if unexpected costs arise.

To optimize costs further, Azure provides several cost-saving strategies and best practices.

One effective strategy is to take advantage of Azure Reserved Virtual Machine Instances.

Reserved Instances allow you to prepay for virtual machines, leading to significant cost savings compared to pay-as-you-go pricing.

By committing to a one-year or three-year term, you can reduce your virtual machine costs while maintaining flexibility.

Azure also offers the Azure Hybrid Benefit program, which enables you to use your existing on-premises Windows Server or SQL Server licenses to reduce the cost of running these workloads in Azure.

This program provides cost savings for organizations with Software Assurance.

Azure Cost Management and Billing provide recommendations and cost-saving opportunities tailored to your specific usage patterns.

These recommendations can help you identify opportunities to optimize your resources and reduce your spending.

For example, you may receive recommendations to resize virtual machines, delete unused resources, or switch to lower-cost Azure services.

Implementing these recommendations can lead to immediate cost savings without sacrificing performance or functionality.

Resource tagging is another cost control best practice in Azure.

By assigning tags to your resources, you can categorize and organize them based on various criteria, such as departments, projects, or cost centers.

Tags enable you to track and allocate costs accurately, making it easier to understand which teams or projects are consuming resources and how much they are spending.

Cost allocation based on tags also simplifies chargeback or showback processes within your organization.

To achieve long-term cost control in Azure, it's crucial to establish a culture of cost awareness and accountability within your organization.

This involves educating your teams about Azure cost management best practices and encouraging them to monitor their resource usage regularly.

By involving stakeholders from different departments, you can promote a sense of ownership and responsibility for cost control.

Azure Policy is a valuable tool for enforcing cost control policies and governance within your Azure environment.

With Azure Policy, you can define rules and constraints that help ensure compliance with your organization's spending guidelines.

For example, you can create policies that prevent the deployment of expensive virtual machine sizes or enforce naming conventions to simplify cost allocation.

Azure Cost Management and Billing provide detailed cost breakdowns by resource, service, and location, helping you identify cost optimization opportunities.

For example, you may discover that a specific virtual machine size or storage account type is driving a significant portion of your costs.

By optimizing these resources, you can achieve substantial cost savings.

Another effective cost control strategy is leveraging Azure Spot Virtual Machines.

Spot Virtual Machines allow you to take advantage of unused Azure capacity at a significantly lower cost.

While Spot Virtual Machines offer cost savings, they come with the understanding that Azure may preemptively reclaim the virtual machines if capacity becomes scarce.

Therefore, they are best suited for workloads that can tolerate interruptions or are fault-tolerant.

To further optimize your costs, you can use Azure's auto-scaling capabilities.

Auto-scaling allows you to automatically adjust the number of resources based on workload demand.

This ensures that you are not over-provisioning resources during periods of low demand, which can lead to unnecessary costs.

Azure provides several services, such as Azure Application Insights and Azure Monitor, to help you gain insights into your application's performance and resource utilization.

By analyzing these insights, you can make data-driven decisions to rightsize your resources and achieve cost savings.

In summary, cost control and budgeting in Azure are essential for organizations looking to optimize their cloud spending and align it with their business goals.

Azure offers a range of tools, best practices, and strategies to help you manage costs effectively.

By leveraging Azure Cost Management and Billing, setting up budgets and alerts, implementing cost-saving strategies, and promoting a cost-aware culture within your organization, you can achieve long-term cost control and maximize the value of your Azure investments.

Resource tagging and cost allocation strategies play a crucial role in managing the finances of an organization's cloud resources.

Tagging is a method of attaching metadata or labels to cloud resources, allowing for easy categorization, organization, and allocation of costs.

By assigning tags to resources, organizations can gain visibility into how their cloud spending is distributed across different departments, projects, or cost centers.

This visibility enables more accurate cost allocation, budgeting, and financial accountability.

One common approach to resource tagging is to use tags based on the purpose or owner of the resource.

For example, resources can be tagged with labels like "marketing," "development," "production," or "finance" to indicate the department responsible for those resources.

Additionally, tags can specify the project or application associated with the resource, providing granular insights into where cloud expenses are allocated.

By following a consistent and well-defined tagging strategy, organizations can create a structured taxonomy that simplifies cost allocation and reporting.

Azure, for instance, supports user-defined tags that can be applied to various resource types, including virtual machines, storage accounts, and databases.

These tags can be assigned and managed through the Azure portal, Azure PowerShell, Azure CLI, or various automation tools.

Azure Cost Management and Billing provide robust tools for tracking and analyzing spending based on resource tags.

With these tools, organizations can generate detailed reports and cost breakdowns that show how resources are distributed across different tags and categories.

This information empowers financial teams to allocate costs accurately to the respective departments or projects, facilitating transparent financial reporting and chargeback.

Resource tagging also supports the identification of cost optimization opportunities.

By examining cost breakdowns by tag, organizations can pinpoint areas of overspending or inefficiency.

For instance, if a particular department consistently incurs higher cloud costs, it may prompt further investigation into resource optimization or cost containment measures.

Resource tagging and cost allocation strategies become even more critical in multi-cloud environments.

Many organizations use a combination of cloud providers like Azure, AWS, and Google Cloud to meet their diverse computing needs.

In such scenarios, it becomes challenging to manage and allocate costs accurately without a robust tagging strategy.

Consistency in tagging practices across different cloud platforms allows organizations to maintain a unified approach to cost allocation and reporting.

To implement effective resource tagging and cost allocation, organizations should establish clear policies and guidelines for tagging resources.

These policies should specify the naming conventions, tag categories, and definitions to ensure consistency.

Education and training for cloud users and administrators are also essential to ensure that tagging practices are followed consistently.

Automation can play a significant role in enforcing tagging policies.

By using automation scripts or deployment templates, organizations can ensure that resources are tagged correctly during provisioning.

Azure Policy, for example, can be used to enforce tagging requirements and prevent the deployment of resources without the required tags.

Organizations can also implement role-based access control (RBAC) to restrict access to tagging-related operations.

This ensures that only authorized personnel can create, modify, or delete tags, reducing the risk of mismanagement or tag misuse.

Cost allocation is closely tied to resource tagging.

Once resources are appropriately tagged, organizations can implement cost allocation processes that align with their business goals.

For example, organizations may allocate cloud costs based on usage, a fixed percentage, or a combination of both.

Usage-based allocation methods distribute costs according to the actual consumption of resources.

This method is suitable for scenarios where different departments or projects have varying levels of resource utilization.

Fixed-percentage allocation methods assign a predetermined percentage of costs to each department or project, regardless of actual usage.

This approach provides predictable cost allocation but may not reflect actual resource consumption accurately.

Hybrid allocation methods combine both usage-based and fixed-percentage allocation.

For instance, an organization may allocate a fixed percentage of costs for shared infrastructure resources while using usage-based allocation for application-specific resources.

Azure Cost Management and Billing allow organizations to define cost allocation rules based on tags and other criteria.

These rules automate the allocation process, ensuring that costs are distributed accurately across tagged resources.

Regular review and adjustment of cost allocation methods are essential to adapt to changing business needs.

As organizations evolve, their cost allocation strategies may need to be refined to reflect new departments, projects, or resource patterns.

Cost allocation also extends to external customers or clients in scenarios where organizations provide cloud services to customers.

In such cases, clear cost allocation methodologies must be established to determine how cloud costs are passed on to customers, whether through subscription-based pricing, pay-as-you-go models, or other billing arrangements.

Resource tagging and cost allocation are not static processes but rather ongoing practices that require continuous monitoring and optimization.

Regularly reviewing cost allocation reports, adjusting tagging practices, and fine-tuning allocation methods ensure that organizations maintain control over their cloud expenses.

By implementing robust resource tagging and cost allocation strategies, organizations can gain insight into their cloud spending, allocate costs accurately, optimize resources, and make informed financial decisions in the dynamic world of cloud computing.

Chapter 10: Enterprise Case Studies: Real-World Architectures

In this case study, we will explore the journey of a fictional organization, Acme Corporation, as they embark on the process of migrating their legacy systems to Microsoft Azure. Acme Corporation, a well-established manufacturing company, faced the challenge of modernizing their IT infrastructure to stay competitive in a rapidly evolving business landscape.

Their existing legacy systems, some of which had been in use for decades, were becoming increasingly costly to maintain, lacked scalability, and hindered innovation.

Recognizing the need for a strategic IT transformation, Acme Corporation decided to leverage the cloud capabilities of Microsoft Azure to migrate their legacy systems to a more flexible and scalable environment.

The first step in Acme's migration journey was to conduct a comprehensive assessment of their existing IT infrastructure. This assessment involved identifying all legacy systems, understanding their dependencies, and evaluating their compatibility with the cloud.

Acme's IT team collaborated with Azure experts to perform a thorough analysis of their on-premises servers, applications, and databases.

This assessment revealed that Acme had a mix of Windows and Linux servers running various workloads, including manufacturing process control, inventory management, and financial systems.

The assessment also identified potential challenges, such as legacy applications that were tightly coupled with on-premises hardware and custom configurations.

Based on the assessment findings, Acme formulated a migration strategy that prioritized the migration of less complex and critical workloads first.

This phased approach allowed them to gain experience with Azure while minimizing disruption to their daily operations.

Acme decided to start by migrating their web applications and development environments to Azure App Service, a platform-as-a-service (PaaS) offering that simplifies application hosting and scaling.

The IT team used Azure Site Recovery to replicate their virtual machines (VMs) to Azure, ensuring minimal downtime during the migration.

This proved to be a successful strategy, as it allowed Acme to quickly experience the benefits of Azure's scalability and reduced infrastructure management overhead.

The next phase of Acme's migration involved moving their critical manufacturing process control systems to Azure.

These systems were the backbone of Acme's production operations, so the migration had to be meticulously planned and executed.

To ensure a smooth transition, Acme engaged Azure experts to provide guidance on optimizing their manufacturing applications for the cloud.

They adopted Azure Virtual Machines to run these applications, taking advantage of Azure's high availability and disaster recovery capabilities to enhance the reliability of their manufacturing processes.

Acme also implemented Azure IoT services to collect real-time data from their production lines, allowing them to gain insights into performance and efficiency.

The migration of their manufacturing systems marked a significant milestone in Acme's cloud journey, enabling them to achieve greater agility and responsiveness in their operations.

As Acme continued to migrate their legacy systems, they encountered challenges related to data migration and integration.

Many of their existing databases and data warehouses had complex schemas and dependencies that required careful planning.

To address these challenges, Acme utilized Azure Database Migration Service to migrate their on-premises databases to Azure SQL Database.

They also leveraged Azure Data Factory to orchestrate and automate data integration workflows, ensuring that data remained accessible and consistent throughout the migration process.

Acme's migration journey also involved optimizing their cost management and governance practices in Azure.

They implemented Azure Cost Management and Billing to gain visibility into their cloud spending and track expenses associated with each migrated workload.

By setting up cost allocation based on resource tags, Acme could accurately allocate cloud costs to different departments and projects, improving financial transparency and accountability.

As they continued their migration efforts, Acme embraced Azure DevOps practices to streamline their application development and deployment processes.

They adopted continuous integration and continuous deployment (CI/CD) pipelines, enabling faster and more reliable software releases.

This approach allowed Acme to iterate and innovate more rapidly, responding to market demands with agility.

Throughout their migration journey, Acme Corporation prioritized security and compliance in Azure.

They implemented Azure Security Center to enhance threat detection and response, ensuring the protection of their sensitive data and intellectual property.

Acme also aligned with industry-specific compliance standards, leveraging Azure's compliance offerings to meet regulatory requirements in their manufacturing sector.

The successful migration of their legacy systems to Azure not only improved Acme's IT infrastructure but also transformed their business operations.

With the flexibility and scalability of Azure, Acme could adjust resources on-demand, accommodating seasonal fluctuations in manufacturing demand efficiently.

The enhanced data analytics capabilities provided them with insights that led to better decision-making, reduced production costs, and increased product quality.

In summary, Acme Corporation's migration of legacy systems to Microsoft Azure was a strategic move that revitalized their IT infrastructure and empowered them to remain competitive in a rapidly changing business landscape.

By conducting thorough assessments, prioritizing workloads, optimizing data management, embracing cost management practices, and focusing on security and compliance, Acme achieved a successful migration that delivered tangible benefits to their operations and positioned them for future growth and innovation in the cloud era.

In this case study, we will delve into the journey of a fictional startup, TechSprint, as they leverage Microsoft Azure to build scalable web applications that can handle rapid growth and demand.

TechSprint, a dynamic technology company, aspired to create innovative web applications that could quickly respond to user demands and scale seamlessly as their user base expanded.

Recognizing the need for a robust and scalable cloud platform, TechSprint turned to Microsoft Azure to meet their requirements.

The first step in TechSprint's journey was to conceptualize and design their web applications, taking into account Azure's capabilities for scalability and resilience.

They worked closely with Azure solution architects to create a comprehensive architecture that leveraged Azure's services and features effectively.

TechSprint's web applications were designed to serve a wide range of users, from individuals to enterprises, making scalability a top priority.

To achieve this, they adopted Azure App Service, a platform-as-a-service (PaaS) offering, to host their web applications.

Azure App Service provided a managed environment for deploying and scaling web apps, allowing TechSprint to focus on development rather than infrastructure management.

TechSprint also embraced microservices architecture, breaking down their applications into smaller, independently deployable components.

This approach allowed them to scale individual services independently, optimizing resource utilization and cost efficiency.

To ensure high availability and fault tolerance, TechSprint deployed their web applications across multiple Azure regions, leveraging Azure Traffic Manager for global load balancing.

This multi-region deployment strategy not only improved application availability but also reduced the risk of downtime due to regional outages.

TechSprint also recognized the importance of data storage and management in their web applications.

They employed Azure Cosmos DB, a globally distributed, multi-model database service, to store and retrieve user data efficiently.

Azure Cosmos DB's ability to scale horizontally and globally made it an ideal choice for TechSprint's data-intensive applications.

TechSprint's developers embraced Azure DevOps practices to streamline their development and deployment processes.

They implemented continuous integration and continuous deployment (CI/CD) pipelines using Azure DevOps Services, enabling automated testing and deployment of code changes.

This automation accelerated the release cycle, allowing TechSprint to deliver new features and updates to their users faster.

As TechSprint's user base grew, they faced the challenge of managing increasing amounts of user-generated content and media files.

To address this, they utilized Azure Blob Storage for cost-effective and scalable storage of binary large objects (BLOBs).

Azure Blob Storage's geo-replication and redundancy options ensured data durability and availability even in the face of unexpected failures.

TechSprint also integrated Azure Content Delivery Network (CDN) into their applications to improve the delivery of media assets to users worldwide.

This CDN optimization reduced latency and improved the user experience, especially for global users accessing TechSprint's applications.

In terms of security, TechSprint prioritized Azure's built-in security features.

They implemented Azure Active Directory (Azure AD) for identity and access management, enabling secure authentication and authorization for their users.

Azure Key Vault was used to securely store and manage sensitive application secrets and cryptographic keys.

TechSprint also implemented Azure Security Center to monitor and respond to security threats proactively.

The real-time threat detection and automated security recommendations provided by Azure Security Center ensured that TechSprint's web applications remained resilient against potential attacks.

As TechSprint continued to scale their web applications, they monitored their Azure resources closely to optimize costs.

They leveraged Azure Cost Management and Billing to gain insights into their cloud spending and identify opportunities for cost savings.

By setting up cost alerts and budgets, TechSprint was able to manage their cloud expenses effectively and prevent unexpected overruns.

TechSprint's journey with Azure led to the successful development and deployment of highly scalable web applications.

They were able to handle rapid user growth and spikes in demand without experiencing performance degradation or downtime.

The multi-region deployment, microservices architecture, and use of Azure services allowed TechSprint to achieve high availability and fault tolerance.

TechSprint's applications were responsive and delivered an excellent user experience, thanks to Azure's global infrastructure and Content Delivery Network.

Their commitment to security and compliance ensured that user data remained protected, and their applications were resilient against threats.

TechSprint's embrace of Azure DevOps practices accelerated their development cycles and enabled them to iterate and innovate rapidly.

Through Azure's robust monitoring and cost management tools, TechSprint maintained control over their cloud expenses and optimized their resource usage.

In summary, TechSprint's journey with Azure demonstrated the power of the cloud in building scalable web applications that can adapt to evolving user demands and deliver exceptional performance and reliability.

By leveraging Azure's services, architecture best practices, and a strong focus on security and cost management, TechSprint achieved their goal of creating innovative web applications that could thrive in a dynamic and competitive digital landscape.

Book 4
IaaS Expertise
Harnessing the Power of IBM Cloud for Enterprise Solutions

ROB BOTWRIGHT

Chapter 1: The Significance of IBM Cloud in Enterprise IaaS

Large enterprises today are faced with complex challenges and evolving technology landscapes, making it imperative to consider the advantages of IBM Cloud in their digital transformation journey.

One of the key advantages of IBM Cloud for large enterprises is its robust hybrid cloud capabilities, allowing organizations to seamlessly integrate on-premises infrastructure with cloud resources.

This hybrid approach provides the flexibility to scale resources up or down as needed, ensuring that enterprises can meet fluctuating demands without overprovisioning.

IBM Cloud also offers a wide range of cloud services and solutions tailored to the needs of large enterprises, from advanced analytics to artificial intelligence and machine learning, enabling organizations to harness the power of data and drive innovation.

For enterprises with stringent regulatory and compliance requirements, IBM Cloud provides a secure and compliant environment, including certifications such as ISO 27001 and SOC 2, which are essential for industries like healthcare and finance.

Furthermore, IBM Cloud's robust security features, including encryption, identity and access management, and threat detection, help large enterprises protect their sensitive data and maintain trust with their customers.

IBM's global network of data centers ensures low-latency access to cloud resources from anywhere in the world, making it suitable for large enterprises with a global presence.

The scalability of IBM Cloud allows enterprises to grow their infrastructure in line with business expansion, ensuring that IT resources are aligned with organizational goals.

Large enterprises often require high-performance computing capabilities, and IBM Cloud offers solutions that cater to these needs, enabling complex simulations, data analysis, and scientific research.

IBM's expertise in hybrid cloud management and automation tools simplifies the management of large and complex cloud environments, reducing operational overhead and allowing IT teams to focus on strategic initiatives.

The flexibility of IBM Cloud's pricing models, including pay-as-you-go and reserved instances, allows enterprises to optimize costs while maintaining the agility to adapt to changing market conditions.

In addition to infrastructure and platform services, IBM Cloud provides a marketplace of third-party applications and services that can accelerate development and innovation for large enterprises.

The partnership between IBM and Red Hat, which offers OpenShift container orchestration, enables large enterprises to build and manage containerized applications across hybrid and multicloud environments.

IBM Cloud also supports DevOps practices, facilitating collaboration between development and operations teams to accelerate application delivery and improve software quality.

For large enterprises engaged in AI and machine learning initiatives, IBM Cloud's Watson services offer advanced capabilities for natural language processing, computer vision, and predictive analytics.

IBM Cloud's comprehensive suite of cloud solutions includes cloud storage, database management, and serverless computing, providing large enterprises with the tools they need to modernize their IT infrastructure.

With IBM Cloud's global reach, enterprises can deploy applications and services close to their customers, reducing latency and enhancing user experiences.

IBM's commitment to open standards and interoperability ensures that large enterprises can avoid vendor lock-in and maintain flexibility in their cloud strategy.

IBM Cloud also offers robust disaster recovery and business continuity solutions, helping large enterprises minimize downtime and data loss in the event of a disaster or outage.

Moreover, IBM Cloud's support for edge computing enables large enterprises to process data closer to the source, making it suitable for applications like IoT and real-time analytics.

As large enterprises embark on their cloud journey, the advantages of IBM Cloud become evident in its ability to deliver a secure, scalable, and innovative platform that supports their digital transformation efforts.

With a focus on hybrid cloud, compliance, security, high performance, and flexibility, IBM Cloud empowers large enterprises to stay competitive in today's rapidly evolving business landscape.

By leveraging IBM Cloud's comprehensive suite of services, organizations can drive efficiency, enhance customer experiences, and accelerate their journey toward becoming digitally transformed enterprises.

In the era of digital transformation, businesses across various industries are turning to cloud computing as a pivotal component, and IBM Cloud plays a significant role in this transformative journey.

One of the fundamental aspects of IBM Cloud's role in digital transformation is its ability to provide organizations with the agility and scalability needed to adapt to rapidly changing market dynamics.

By leveraging cloud resources, businesses can quickly scale their infrastructure up or down to meet fluctuating demand, enabling them to respond more effectively to customer needs.

IBM Cloud's hybrid cloud capabilities further enhance its role in digital transformation, allowing organizations to seamlessly integrate their existing on-premises infrastructure with cloud resources.

This hybrid approach enables a gradual migration to the cloud, preserving investments in legacy systems while taking advantage of the cloud's innovation potential.

Furthermore, IBM Cloud provides a rich set of cloud services and solutions that empower businesses to leverage advanced technologies such as artificial intelligence (AI), machine learning (ML), and data analytics.

These capabilities enable organizations to derive valuable insights from their data, automate processes, and gain a competitive edge in their respective markets.

For businesses seeking to improve their decision-making processes, IBM Cloud's AI-powered services, including IBM Watson, offer natural language understanding, sentiment analysis, and predictive analytics, allowing them to make data-driven decisions.

Security and compliance are paramount in the digital age, and IBM Cloud plays a vital role in addressing these concerns.

IBM Cloud's robust security features, including encryption, identity and access management, and threat detection, help organizations protect their sensitive data and maintain regulatory compliance.

This is particularly crucial for industries with stringent compliance requirements, such as healthcare and finance.

IBM Cloud's global network of data centers ensures low-latency access to cloud resources from anywhere in the world, which is essential for businesses with a global presence.

This global reach enables organizations to deliver a consistent and responsive experience to their customers and users, regardless of their geographic location.

The scalability of IBM Cloud is another critical aspect of its role in digital transformation, as it allows organizations to align their IT resources with their business growth.

Large enterprises can expand their infrastructure to accommodate increased workloads and customer demands, while startups and small businesses can start with minimal resources and scale up as they grow.

In terms of cost management, IBM Cloud offers flexible pricing models, including pay-as-you-go and reserved instances, allowing organizations to optimize their cloud spending.

This flexibility ensures that businesses can manage their IT budgets effectively while remaining agile in their operations.

Moreover, IBM Cloud provides a marketplace of third-party applications and services that complement its core offerings, enabling organizations to access a wide range of solutions to accelerate their digital transformation initiatives.

The partnership between IBM and Red Hat, which includes offerings such as OpenShift for container orchestration, simplifies the development and management of applications across hybrid and multicloud environments.

IBM Cloud's support for DevOps practices facilitates collaboration between development and operations teams, streamlining application delivery and enhancing software quality.

This approach empowers organizations to iterate and innovate more rapidly, respond to market changes quickly, and stay competitive.

For businesses engaged in AI and ML projects, IBM Cloud's Watson services provide a robust platform for building and deploying AI-driven applications.

These services encompass natural language processing, computer vision, and predictive analytics, enabling organizations to harness the power of AI to solve complex business challenges.

IBM Cloud's extensive suite of cloud solutions includes cloud storage, database management, and serverless computing, providing organizations with the tools they need to modernize their IT infrastructure and innovate.

In summary, IBM Cloud plays a pivotal role in digital transformation by offering organizations the essential components needed to thrive in the digital age.

From hybrid cloud capabilities and advanced technologies to security and compliance features, IBM Cloud empowers businesses to adapt, innovate, and drive growth in today's rapidly evolving business landscape.

By embracing IBM Cloud, organizations can embark on a transformative journey that enables them to stay competitive, deliver exceptional customer experiences, and achieve their digital transformation goals.

Chapter 2: Navigating the IBM Cloud Infrastructure Landscape

To comprehend the scope and significance of IBM Cloud's global infrastructure, it's crucial to delve into the intricacies of its data centers and regions.

IBM Cloud boasts an extensive network of data centers strategically located in regions around the world, forming the backbone of its cloud services.

These data centers serve as the physical foundation that hosts the virtualized computing resources and storage, making them vital components of the cloud ecosystem.

One of the primary reasons for the distributed nature of data centers is to ensure low-latency access to cloud resources for users and businesses in various geographic locations.

By having data centers in proximity to end-users, IBM Cloud minimizes the time it takes for data to travel between users and cloud resources, resulting in faster response times and improved user experiences.

Furthermore, the global network of data centers plays a critical role in disaster recovery and business continuity planning.

In the event of an outage or disaster in one region, workloads and data can be seamlessly shifted to data centers in other regions, reducing the risk of downtime and data loss.

IBM Cloud's commitment to redundancy and failover mechanisms within its data centers contributes to the high availability and reliability of its cloud services.

Each data center is designed with redundant power sources, network connectivity, and cooling systems to ensure uninterrupted operation.

Moreover, data centers are equipped with advanced monitoring and security systems to protect against physical threats and unauthorized access.

IBM Cloud strategically selects regions for data center deployment based on factors such as customer demand, regulatory requirements, and emerging markets.

These regions are typically composed of multiple data centers that work in tandem to provide high availability and load balancing.

For example, IBM Cloud's regions in North America may include data centers in locations such as Dallas, Toronto, and Washington, D.C., among others.

In Europe, regions may encompass data centers in London, Frankfurt, and Amsterdam, to name a few.

Asia-Pacific regions may have data centers in Tokyo, Singapore, and Sydney, while Latin America could include data centers in São Paulo and Mexico City.

Each region serves as a localized hub for cloud services, allowing organizations to choose the region that best suits their data residency and latency requirements.

Customers can deploy their applications and store their data within a specific region to comply with data sovereignty regulations or optimize performance.

IBM Cloud's regions are interconnected through a global network infrastructure, enabling data replication and redundancy across regions for added resilience.

This interconnectedness also facilitates data transfer and workload migration between regions, giving organizations the flexibility to scale their resources globally.

IBM Cloud continuously expands its global footprint by adding new regions and data centers to meet the growing demand for cloud services.

This expansion strategy reflects IBM Cloud's commitment to providing businesses with the resources and capabilities they need to innovate and grow.

The availability of multiple regions and data centers within each region allows organizations to implement geographically distributed architectures for high availability and disaster recovery.

For instance, a business could deploy its primary application infrastructure in one region and replicate it in another for failover purposes.

This approach ensures that the organization can maintain uninterrupted operations even in the face of regional outages or disasters.

Moreover, the global network of data centers enables businesses to adopt multicloud and hybrid cloud strategies.

They can use IBM Cloud's resources in conjunction with their on-premises infrastructure or other cloud providers, creating a flexible and interoperable environment.

IBM Cloud's data center infrastructure is underpinned by a commitment to sustainability and environmental responsibility.

Efforts are made to optimize energy efficiency within data centers, reduce carbon emissions, and minimize the environmental impact of operations.

This commitment aligns with the growing emphasis on eco-friendly practices and corporate social responsibility in the technology industry.

In summary, understanding IBM Cloud's data centers and regions is pivotal to grasping the scale and capability of its global cloud infrastructure.

These data centers serve as the physical foundation for its cloud services, providing low-latency access, high availability, and disaster recovery capabilities.

IBM Cloud's distributed network of data centers allows organizations to tailor their cloud deployments to meet their specific needs, whether it be data residency, performance optimization, or disaster resilience.

The interconnectedness of these data centers enables global resource scalability and supports multicloud and hybrid cloud strategies.

By expanding its global footprint and adhering to sustainability principles, IBM Cloud remains at the forefront of cloud infrastructure providers, offering businesses the tools they need to thrive in an increasingly digital and interconnected world.

Selecting the appropriate IBM Cloud infrastructure services is a crucial decision that can significantly impact an organization's ability to achieve its goals in the digital age.

IBM Cloud offers a diverse range of infrastructure services, each designed to cater to specific use cases and business requirements.

To make an informed choice, it's essential to understand the options available and match them with your organization's needs.

One fundamental infrastructure service offered by IBM Cloud is virtual servers, which provide scalable compute resources in the form of virtual machines (VMs).

These VMs can be provisioned with various operating systems and configurations, making them suitable for running applications, hosting websites, or conducting development and testing.

IBM Cloud's virtual servers offer flexibility, allowing organizations to adjust resources as demands change, whether it's increasing CPU and memory for peak workloads or reducing them during off-peak times.

For businesses that require a higher level of control over their infrastructure, IBM Cloud offers bare metal servers.

These physical servers provide dedicated resources and allow organizations to install and manage their preferred operating systems and software.

Bare metal servers are well-suited for demanding workloads, such as high-performance computing, large-scale databases, and specialized applications that require direct hardware access.

IBM Cloud's container service, powered by Kubernetes, enables organizations to orchestrate and manage containerized applications efficiently.

Containers offer a lightweight and portable way to package and deploy applications, making it easier to move workloads between environments and streamline the development process.

The Kubernetes-based container service provides features like automatic scaling, load balancing, and rolling updates, simplifying the management of containerized applications.

Another infrastructure service in IBM Cloud's portfolio is cloud storage, which encompasses various options, including block storage, file storage, and object storage.

Block storage is suitable for hosting databases and applications that require high-performance and low-latency access to data.

File storage is designed for sharing files across multiple instances and is ideal for applications that rely on a centralized file system.

Object storage, on the other hand, is suitable for storing vast amounts of unstructured data, such as backups, media files, and documents.

IBM Cloud's object storage service offers scalability, data durability, and a straightforward pricing model, making it a cost-effective choice for storing large volumes of data.

For organizations seeking a fully managed database solution, IBM Cloud offers database services for various database engines, including Db2, PostgreSQL, MySQL, and MongoDB.

These managed database services handle tasks such as provisioning, patching, and backups, allowing organizations to focus on application development rather than database administration.

Additionally, IBM Cloud provides database migration services to simplify the transition of existing on-premises databases to the cloud.

IBM Cloud also offers a content delivery network (CDN) service that helps organizations accelerate the delivery of web content and applications to end-users around the world.

By caching and distributing content from strategically located edge servers, CDN services reduce latency and improve the performance of websites and applications, enhancing the user experience.

When it comes to networking, IBM Cloud provides a wide range of options, including virtual private clouds (VPCs), load balancers, and security groups.

VPCs allow organizations to create isolated network environments with granular control over IP addressing, routing, and security policies.

Load balancers distribute incoming traffic across multiple instances, ensuring high availability and improved fault tolerance for applications.

Security groups enable organizations to define network access controls, specifying which traffic is allowed or blocked to enhance security.

Furthermore, IBM Cloud offers services for network monitoring, intrusion detection, and distributed denial of service (DDoS) protection to safeguard against cyber threats.

For businesses looking to leverage artificial intelligence and machine learning, IBM Cloud provides a suite of AI and ML services powered by IBM Watson.

These services include natural language understanding, speech recognition, image recognition, and predictive analytics, enabling organizations to incorporate AI-driven capabilities into their applications and processes.

IBM Cloud's AI and ML services facilitate tasks such as sentiment analysis, chatbot development, and anomaly detection, unlocking new opportunities for innovation and automation.

In addition to these infrastructure services, IBM Cloud offers a wide array of management and DevOps tools to streamline operations and enhance developer productivity.

These tools encompass continuous integration and continuous delivery (CI/CD), monitoring, logging, and resource management capabilities.

Choosing the right IBM Cloud infrastructure services involves evaluating your organization's specific requirements, such as performance, scalability, security, and compliance.

It's essential to consider factors like application architecture, data storage needs, geographic distribution, and budget constraints when making decisions.

Collaboration among IT, development, and business teams is critical to aligning infrastructure choices with organizational goals and ensuring that the selected services support your digital transformation initiatives effectively.

Furthermore, organizations should remain adaptable, as technology and business requirements evolve over time.

Regularly assessing your infrastructure needs and adjusting your usage of IBM Cloud services can help optimize costs, improve agility, and stay competitive in a rapidly changing digital landscape.

In summary, the right choice of IBM Cloud infrastructure services can be a catalyst for an organization's digital success.

By understanding the available options and aligning them with your specific needs and objectives, you can leverage IBM Cloud's capabilities to innovate, grow, and thrive in the digital era.

Chapter 3: Networking Strategies for Enterprise Cloud Solution

Understanding IBM Cloud networking basics and best practices is essential for organizations seeking to harness the full potential of the cloud environment for their digital initiatives.

IBM Cloud offers a robust and flexible network infrastructure that can be tailored to meet the unique requirements of various applications and workloads.

At its core, IBM Cloud networking is built on a foundation of virtual private clouds (VPCs), which provide a secure and isolated network environment for resources and services.

VPCs allow organizations to define their own IP address ranges, subnets, and routing policies, granting them full control over their network architecture.

One of the fundamental best practices in IBM Cloud networking is to design your VPCs with security in mind, implementing strict access controls and isolation of resources to minimize attack surfaces.

By using security groups and network access controls, organizations can control inbound and outbound traffic, ensuring that only authorized communication occurs within the VPC.

Furthermore, the concept of isolation extends to the use of multiple VPCs for different purposes, such as development, testing, and production, to prevent cross-environment contamination.

To ensure optimal network performance and reliability, IBM Cloud offers load balancing services that distribute incoming traffic across multiple instances or resources.

Load balancers are essential for high availability and fault tolerance, as they can automatically reroute traffic in case of instance failures, reducing downtime.

When configuring load balancers, it's crucial to consider factors like session persistence and health checks to guarantee seamless user experiences and application availability.

In addition to load balancing, organizations can leverage content delivery network (CDN) services provided by IBM Cloud to accelerate the delivery of web content and applications to end-users worldwide.

CDN services cache and distribute content from edge servers strategically located across the globe, reducing latency and improving response times for users accessing web applications and content.

Another critical aspect of IBM Cloud networking is the establishment of secure and high-performance connections between on-premises data centers and IBM Cloud resources.

IBM Cloud offers dedicated network connections through services like Direct Link, which provides private, low-latency connections to the cloud.

Additionally, VPN services enable organizations to create encrypted tunnels over the public internet to securely extend their on-premises networks into the cloud.

These connectivity options are vital for hybrid cloud deployments, ensuring seamless integration between on-premises and cloud-based resources.

For organizations with geographically dispersed users and resources, IBM Cloud's global network of data centers and regions offers an advantage.

By strategically deploying resources in the region closest to their users, organizations can minimize latency and optimize network performance.

This regional approach is particularly beneficial for applications that demand low-latency interactions, such as real-time gaming, video streaming, and financial trading platforms.

To enhance network visibility and troubleshooting capabilities, IBM Cloud provides network monitoring and logging services.

These services enable organizations to track and analyze network traffic, detect anomalies, and troubleshoot connectivity issues effectively.

By utilizing these monitoring tools, organizations can proactively identify and address potential network bottlenecks or security incidents.

Furthermore, organizations should consider implementing distributed denial of service (DDoS) protection services offered by IBM Cloud to safeguard against cyber threats.

DDoS protection services can automatically detect and mitigate large-scale DDoS attacks, ensuring uninterrupted availability of cloud resources.

To optimize network performance and cost, organizations can explore IBM Cloud's global load balancing and traffic steering capabilities.

These features allow organizations to direct traffic to the most suitable data center or region based on factors like latency, availability, and cost.

This approach helps organizations achieve optimal performance while managing network costs effectively.

As organizations increasingly adopt multicloud and hybrid cloud strategies, IBM Cloud's networking capabilities support interoperability and connectivity with other cloud providers.

This interoperability enables organizations to create a seamless and interconnected cloud environment that spans multiple cloud platforms while maintaining consistent network policies and security controls.

When it comes to network security, IBM Cloud emphasizes the importance of encryption, both in transit and at rest.

Organizations should employ encryption protocols, such as SSL/TLS, to secure data in transit between users and cloud resources.

Additionally, encryption should be applied to data stored in cloud services to protect sensitive information from unauthorized access.

Regularly updating security certificates and encryption keys is another best practice to ensure the continued security of data and communications.

To maximize network resilience, organizations should consider redundancy and failover strategies when designing their network architecture.

Redundant components, such as multiple internet connections and load balancers, can help maintain network availability even in the event of component failures.

Creating backup routes and failover mechanisms ensures that traffic can be rerouted seamlessly in case of network disruptions.

Finally, organizations should continuously monitor and audit their network configurations and security policies to identify vulnerabilities and compliance issues.

Regular assessments and proactive adjustments help maintain a secure and well-optimized network infrastructure in IBM Cloud.

In summary, IBM Cloud networking basics and best practices are essential for organizations looking to harness the full potential of cloud technology.

By understanding and implementing these principles, organizations can create a secure, high-performance, and resilient network environment that supports their digital initiatives and growth in the cloud era.

Establishing secure VPN (Virtual Private Network) and Direct Link connections is a critical aspect of modern networking, enabling organizations to securely extend their on-premises networks to the cloud.

VPNs provide a secure and encrypted communication channel over the public internet, allowing remote users or branch offices to connect to a private network, such as a corporate intranet.

One key advantage of VPNs is their ability to create secure tunnels that protect data from eavesdropping and tampering while in transit.

Organizations can implement VPNs to facilitate secure remote access for employees or to interconnect multiple locations.

However, it's essential to choose the right VPN technology and configuration to meet your organization's specific needs.

Site-to-site VPNs connect two or more networks, typically linking a corporate data center to a cloud-based infrastructure.

These connections enable seamless communication between on-premises resources and cloud resources, extending the organization's network perimeter to the cloud.

Remote access VPNs, on the other hand, provide individual users or remote offices with secure access to the corporate network over the internet.

Organizations can use remote access VPNs to facilitate secure remote work or access to resources hosted in the cloud.

When implementing VPNs, security is paramount, and organizations should adhere to best practices for configuring and managing VPN connections.

This includes using strong encryption protocols, regularly updating VPN software and firmware, and enforcing strict access controls.

To enhance security further, organizations can implement multi-factor authentication (MFA) for VPN access, requiring users to provide multiple forms of authentication, such as a password and a one-time token.

Additionally, VPN logs should be monitored and audited regularly to detect and respond to any suspicious activity or unauthorized access attempts.

Direct Link, provided by cloud providers like IBM Cloud, offers a dedicated and private network connection between an organization's on-premises data center or network and the cloud provider's data center.

Unlike VPNs, which rely on the public internet, Direct Link connections offer a more reliable and predictable network experience.

Direct Link connections can be established with different bandwidth options, ensuring organizations have the necessary capacity to support their workloads and applications.

One of the primary advantages of Direct Link is its ability to offer consistent and low-latency network performance, making it ideal for applications that demand real-time data transfer and low-latency communication.

To establish a Direct Link connection, organizations need to choose a Direct Link provider, such as IBM Cloud, and select the appropriate connection options based on their requirements.

This may include the choice of port speed, connection type (Ethernet or IP VPN), and the selection of the data center location where the connection will terminate.

Once the connection is provisioned, organizations can configure their network equipment to connect to the Direct

Link circuit, creating a dedicated and private link between their on-premises network and the cloud provider's network. It's crucial to ensure that the Direct Link connection is properly secured, which may involve implementing encryption and access controls on the network equipment used for the connection.

Security measures like encryption and access controls should align with the organization's overall security policies and compliance requirements.

In addition to security, organizations should also consider redundancy and failover options when establishing Direct Link connections.

Redundant connections and failover mechanisms help ensure network availability and minimize the risk of disruptions due to hardware failures or network issues.

Direct Link connections can be particularly advantageous for hybrid cloud scenarios, where organizations want to seamlessly integrate their on-premises resources with cloud-based services.

By establishing Direct Link connections, organizations can achieve a high level of network reliability and performance while securely accessing cloud resources.

However, it's essential to monitor the Direct Link connection and regularly assess its performance to identify and address any potential issues or bottlenecks.

To further enhance network security and isolation, organizations can consider the use of Virtual Private Clouds (VPCs) or Virtual LANs (VLANs) in conjunction with Direct Link connections.

VPCs and VLANs allow organizations to create isolated network segments within their cloud environments, enhancing security and traffic separation.

This level of network segmentation helps organizations control access and data flow within their cloud infrastructure.

Moreover, organizations can implement network monitoring and alerting solutions to gain visibility into the performance and health of their Direct Link connections.

Monitoring tools can detect anomalies, track bandwidth utilization, and provide insights into network performance, helping organizations optimize their network resources effectively.

When establishing Direct Link connections, it's essential to work closely with the chosen Direct Link provider to ensure proper configuration and ongoing support.

Providers like IBM Cloud offer resources, documentation, and technical support to assist organizations in setting up and managing their Direct Link connections successfully.

In summary, establishing secure VPN and Direct Link connections is a fundamental component of modern network architecture, enabling organizations to securely and reliably connect their on-premises networks to the cloud.

VPNs offer flexible and encrypted connections over the public internet, while Direct Link provides dedicated and private connections with predictable performance.

By implementing these secure network connections and adhering to best practices, organizations can seamlessly extend their networks to the cloud and leverage the benefits of hybrid cloud environments while maintaining the highest level of security and reliability.

Chapter 4: Leveraging IBM Cloud Virtual Servers for Scalability

In the IBM Cloud ecosystem, virtual servers play a pivotal role in hosting and managing workloads and applications, and understanding the various virtual server types and their configurations is essential for optimizing cloud infrastructure.

IBM Cloud offers a diverse range of virtual server types, each tailored to specific use cases and performance requirements. The most basic virtual server type is known as the "Virtual Server," which provides a balanced mix of CPU, memory, and storage resources, suitable for a wide range of general-purpose applications.

These Virtual Servers can be further customized by choosing from different CPU and memory configurations, allowing organizations to align their resources with the demands of their workloads.

For organizations seeking more performance, the "Balanced Virtual Server" offers a higher CPU-to-memory ratio, making it well-suited for applications that require increased processing power.

Balanced Virtual Servers are available in various CPU and memory configurations to accommodate different workload needs.

On the other hand, the "Memory-Optimized Virtual Server" prioritizes memory capacity over CPU power, making it ideal for memory-intensive applications like in-memory databases or analytics workloads.

Memory-Optimized Virtual Servers come in multiple memory capacity options, ensuring that organizations can select the right balance of resources for their specific requirements.

In scenarios where computational power is the primary focus, the "Compute-Optimized Virtual Server" offers the highest CPU-to-memory ratio, making it suitable for applications that demand significant processing capabilities.

These servers are available with varying CPU configurations to meet the demands of compute-intensive workloads.

For workloads that require a balance between memory and CPU power, the "GPU-Accelerated Virtual Server" integrates graphics processing units (GPUs) to enhance computational performance for tasks like machine learning, AI, or graphics rendering.

GPU-Accelerated Virtual Servers come with GPU options, allowing organizations to choose the appropriate level of GPU acceleration for their applications.

Furthermore, the "Dedicated Virtual Server" type provides dedicated physical resources for increased isolation and performance predictability.

These servers are particularly suitable for mission-critical or compliance-sensitive workloads where resource sharing is not acceptable.

Dedicated Virtual Servers can be customized to align with specific CPU, memory, and storage requirements.

In addition to the various virtual server types, IBM Cloud offers the flexibility to select from different operating systems and configurations.

Organizations can choose from a range of operating systems, including various Linux distributions and Windows Server versions, to best support their application stacks and development environments.

To cater to diverse workloads, IBM Cloud provides the option to add additional storage volumes to virtual servers, ensuring that organizations have the necessary storage capacity to meet their data storage requirements.

These additional volumes can be customized in terms of size and type, such as high-performance SSD or cost-effective SATA drives.

For enhanced data protection and disaster recovery capabilities, organizations can leverage the snapshot and backup features available for virtual servers.

Snapshots allow users to capture a point-in-time image of their virtual server's disk, while backups offer automated and scheduled data protection for added peace of mind.

Moreover, organizations can integrate virtual servers with IBM Cloud Load Balancers to distribute incoming traffic across multiple instances for improved availability and scalability.

Load balancers help ensure uninterrupted service delivery and fault tolerance by intelligently routing traffic to healthy instances.

In terms of network connectivity, IBM Cloud provides options for private and public network interfaces, allowing organizations to configure their virtual servers based on their network architecture and security requirements.

Private network interfaces enable secure communication between virtual servers and other resources within the same Virtual Private Cloud (VPC) environment, while public interfaces enable access to the public internet.

To enhance security, organizations can implement network security groups (NSGs) and firewall rules to control inbound and outbound traffic to their virtual servers.

These security measures help protect virtual servers from unauthorized access and potential security threats.

In summary, IBM Cloud offers a versatile array of virtual server types and configurations to cater to the diverse needs of organizations and their workloads.

From general-purpose servers to memory-optimized and GPU-accelerated options, IBM Cloud provides the flexibility to choose the right virtual server type and tailor it to specific performance and resource requirements.

Coupled with options for different operating systems, storage configurations, and data protection features, organizations can confidently deploy and manage virtual servers in IBM Cloud to support their applications and services with reliability, scalability, and security.

Understanding these virtual server options is crucial for optimizing cloud infrastructure and ensuring that organizations can harness the full potential of IBM Cloud to meet their evolving business needs.

Auto-scaling strategies are essential for efficiently managing dynamic workloads in cloud environments, allowing organizations to automatically adjust their compute resources to match changing demand patterns.

By implementing auto-scaling, organizations can optimize resource utilization, enhance performance, and reduce costs by only allocating resources when needed.

One common approach to auto-scaling is vertical scaling, where organizations increase the capacity of a single instance by adding more CPU, memory, or storage resources.

Vertical scaling is suitable for workloads that require occasional bursts of additional resources but may not be the most cost-effective solution for highly variable workloads.

Horizontal scaling, on the other hand, involves adding or removing instances to distribute the workload across multiple servers.

Horizontal scaling is ideal for workloads that experience frequent fluctuations in demand, as it allows organizations to add or remove resources dynamically.

To implement horizontal scaling effectively, organizations need to define specific scaling policies or rules that dictate when and how additional instances should be added or removed.

These rules can be based on various metrics, such as CPU utilization, memory usage, or network traffic, and organizations can set thresholds that trigger scaling actions.

For example, if CPU utilization exceeds 80% for a specified period, a horizontal scaling policy can be triggered to add more instances to handle the increased workload.

Conversely, if CPU utilization drops below a certain threshold, the policy can instruct the auto-scaling system to remove instances to save on costs.

Auto-scaling can also be combined with load balancing to distribute incoming traffic evenly across multiple instances.

Load balancers play a crucial role in ensuring that auto-scaled instances work seamlessly together to provide high availability and fault tolerance.

Organizations can configure load balancers to perform health checks on instances and direct traffic to healthy instances while avoiding those that may be experiencing issues.

One popular approach to auto-scaling is predictive scaling, where organizations use historical data and machine learning algorithms to forecast future demand and proactively scale resources accordingly.

Predictive scaling allows organizations to avoid underprovisioning or overprovisioning resources, optimizing costs and performance.

Another aspect of auto-scaling is defining cooldown periods, which prevent the system from making rapid and unnecessary scaling adjustments.

Cooldown periods ensure that the system observes the effects of a scaling action before initiating another one, preventing a flurry of scaling activities in response to minor fluctuations.

It's essential to fine-tune the duration of cooldown periods to strike the right balance between responsiveness and stability.

Auto-scaling can be used not only to handle increased demand but also to optimize resource allocation during off-peak periods.

For instance, organizations can set up scaling policies that reduce the number of instances during periods of low activity to save on operational costs.

Auto-scaling can be implemented across various cloud providers, including AWS, Azure, Google Cloud, and IBM Cloud, using their respective auto-scaling services or features.

For example, AWS offers Auto Scaling Groups, which allow organizations to define scaling policies based on CloudWatch metrics and automatically adjust the number of instances in a group.

Azure provides Azure Autoscale, which enables organizations to define scaling rules and schedules to manage virtual machine instances.

Google Cloud offers Managed Instance Groups with auto-healing and auto-updating capabilities, allowing for efficient scaling and maintenance.

IBM Cloud includes Auto Scaling for virtual servers, enabling organizations to create policies based on CPU or memory utilization to scale instances horizontally.

When implementing auto-scaling, organizations should continuously monitor their workloads and review scaling policies to ensure they align with changing demands and business goals.

It's crucial to strike a balance between responsiveness and stability to avoid unnecessary scaling actions that may introduce resource contention or incur additional costs.

Additionally, organizations should consider auto-scaling as part of their broader infrastructure management strategy, incorporating it into their overall cloud architecture and deployment practices.

By doing so, organizations can leverage auto-scaling to optimize resource utilization, enhance workload performance, and achieve cost savings while efficiently managing dynamic workloads in the cloud.

In summary, auto-scaling is a fundamental strategy for managing dynamic workloads in cloud environments, enabling organizations to automatically adjust resources to match changing demand patterns.

Horizontal scaling, vertical scaling, load balancing, and predictive scaling are key techniques used in auto-scaling strategies.

These strategies, when applied effectively, help organizations optimize resource allocation, enhance performance, and reduce costs in response to workload fluctuations.

Moreover, auto-scaling can be integrated into cloud services offered by various providers, making it accessible and adaptable for different cloud architectures.

Continuous monitoring and policy refinement are essential to ensure that auto-scaling remains aligned with changing demands and business objectives.

Overall, auto-scaling is a valuable tool in cloud infrastructure management, providing organizations with the agility and efficiency needed to thrive in dynamic computing environments.

Chapter 5: Data Storage and Management in IBM Cloud

IBM Cloud offers a comprehensive range of storage solutions designed to meet the diverse needs of businesses and organizations, whether they require high-performance storage for critical workloads or cost-effective storage for long-term data retention.

One of the key storage offerings provided by IBM Cloud is IBM Cloud Object Storage, a scalable and durable storage service that is ideal for storing unstructured data such as documents, images, videos, and backups.

IBM Cloud Object Storage is designed to handle massive amounts of data and offers high availability and data durability, making it a reliable choice for businesses with demanding data storage requirements.

This storage service allows organizations to store, manage, and retrieve data through a simple and intuitive interface, making it easy to integrate into existing workflows.

Another important storage solution offered by IBM Cloud is IBM Cloud Block Storage, which provides high-performance block storage that can be attached to virtual servers to support applications and databases that require low-latency access to data.

IBM Cloud Block Storage is designed to deliver consistent performance and is suitable for workloads that demand high I/O operations per second (IOPS) and low latency.

Organizations can choose from different performance tiers based on their specific application requirements, ensuring they have the right level of performance for their workloads.

IBM Cloud File Storage is another storage offering that enables organizations to create highly available and scalable file storage systems in the cloud.

This service is designed to support a wide range of file-based workloads, including file shares for applications, content repositories, and data archives.

IBM Cloud File Storage is fully managed, making it easy for organizations to deploy and scale file storage resources without the need for extensive administrative overhead.

Additionally, IBM Cloud offers IBM Cloud Archive Storage, a cost-effective storage solution designed for long-term data retention and compliance requirements.

This storage class is ideal for archiving data that is infrequently accessed but needs to be retained for regulatory or business purposes.

It provides a lower-cost storage option while still ensuring data durability and availability when needed.

For organizations seeking high-performance block storage with advanced features like data encryption and data replication, IBM Cloud offers IBM Cloud Hyper Protect Storage.

This storage service is designed to meet the security and compliance needs of highly regulated industries, such as finance and healthcare.

It leverages hardware-based security features to protect data at rest and in transit, providing organizations with peace of mind when storing sensitive information in the cloud.

IBM Cloud also provides IBM Cloud Data Lake Storage, a scalable and secure storage solution designed for big data and analytics workloads.

It allows organizations to store and analyze vast amounts of data, making it a valuable resource for data-driven decision-making and advanced analytics projects.

IBM Cloud Data Lake Storage integrates with popular data analytics tools and frameworks, making it easier for data scientists and analysts to access and work with their data.

Furthermore, IBM Cloud offers a variety of storage solutions tailored to specific use cases, such as IBM Cloud VMware Solutions Shared Disks, which provides shared block storage for VMware virtual machines, and IBM Cloud Storage for SAP, designed to support SAP applications and workloads.

Additionally, IBM Cloud provides data migration services to help organizations seamlessly move their data to the cloud, ensuring a smooth transition to the cloud environment.

These services include data transfer appliances and tools designed to simplify and accelerate the migration process.

In summary, IBM Cloud offers a comprehensive portfolio of storage solutions to address the storage needs of businesses and organizations across various industries and use cases.

From high-performance block storage to cost-effective archive storage, IBM Cloud's storage offerings are designed to provide scalability, reliability, and security for data storage in the cloud.

With a focus on data durability, availability, and ease of use, IBM Cloud's storage solutions empower organizations to effectively manage their data and leverage it for business insights and innovation.

Data lifecycle management and backup strategies are critical components of any organization's data management and protection efforts, helping ensure the availability, integrity, and security of data throughout its lifecycle.

Data lifecycle management encompasses the processes and policies governing data from its creation or acquisition through its use, sharing, archiving, and eventual disposal.

Effective data lifecycle management is essential to prevent data loss, minimize risks, and optimize storage resources.

One of the key principles of data lifecycle management is understanding the value and relevance of data at different stages of its lifecycle.

Not all data retains the same level of importance or usefulness over time, so organizations must classify their data based on factors such as business criticality, compliance requirements, and access frequency.

By categorizing data, organizations can apply appropriate management and protection measures to each category, reducing the complexity of data management.

Data classification can also aid in setting retention policies, specifying how long data should be retained and when it should be securely deleted.

These policies should align with regulatory requirements and business needs, ensuring compliance while avoiding unnecessary data storage costs.

An essential aspect of data lifecycle management is data backup and recovery, which involves creating copies of data to safeguard against data loss due to hardware failures, accidental deletions, or other unforeseen events.

Data backup strategies should consider the recovery point objective (RPO) and recovery time objective (RTO) for each category of data.

RPO defines the maximum allowable data loss, while RTO specifies the acceptable downtime for data recovery.

Different types of data may have varying RPO and RTO requirements, with critical data demanding more frequent backups and faster recovery capabilities.

Organizations often implement regular backup schedules, automating the process to ensure data consistency and minimize the risk of human error.

Backup methods can include full backups, incremental backups, and differential backups, each with its advantages and trade-offs.

Full backups capture an entire dataset, while incremental backups store changes made since the last backup.

Differential backups, on the other hand, save changes since the last full backup.

The choice of backup method depends on factors like data volume, backup frequency, and recovery time considerations.

Additionally, organizations should consider the storage location of backups, opting for secure and geographically diverse locations to safeguard against disasters.

Cloud-based backup solutions have gained popularity for their scalability, cost-effectiveness, and ease of management.

Many organizations leverage cloud backup services to protect critical data and ensure offsite redundancy.

Another important aspect of data lifecycle management and backup strategies is data retention and archiving.

Not all data needs to be readily accessible in primary storage, and archiving allows organizations to move less frequently accessed data to more cost-effective storage solutions.

Archiving helps reduce primary storage costs, improve performance, and simplify backup and recovery processes.

Organizations can use data archiving solutions to retain data for compliance, legal, or historical purposes while efficiently managing storage resources.

When implementing data backup and archiving solutions, organizations should prioritize data security.

Encryption should be used to protect data both in transit and at rest, ensuring that unauthorized access is prevented.

Access controls and authentication mechanisms should be in place to restrict access to backup and archived data to authorized personnel only.

Regular testing of data recovery processes is crucial to verify the effectiveness of backup and archiving strategies. Organizations should conduct drills and simulations to ensure that data can be successfully restored within the specified RTO and RPO.

These tests help identify any gaps or issues in the backup and recovery procedures that need to be addressed.

Data lifecycle management and backup strategies should also consider the impact of data growth.

As data volumes increase, organizations may need to scale their storage infrastructure and adjust backup and archiving policies accordingly.

Implementing data deduplication and compression techniques can help optimize storage utilization and reduce backup storage requirements.

Moreover, organizations should keep abreast of evolving technologies and industry best practices in data management and protection.

New technologies such as cloud-native backup solutions and artificial intelligence-driven data management tools are continually emerging, offering more efficient and cost-effective ways to manage and protect data.

In summary, data lifecycle management and backup strategies are fundamental aspects of modern data management and protection.

Organizations must classify data, set retention policies, and implement backup and archiving solutions to ensure data availability, integrity, and security.

By aligning these strategies with business needs and regulatory requirements, organizations can mitigate risks, reduce costs, and effectively manage their data throughout its lifecycle.

Chapter 6: Enterprise Security and Compliance in IBM Cloud

IBM Cloud offers a robust set of security features and tools to help organizations protect their data, applications, and infrastructure in the cloud. One of the key security features of IBM Cloud is Identity and Access Management (IAM), which enables organizations to manage user access and permissions to their cloud resources. IAM allows organizations to define roles, permissions, and access policies, ensuring that only authorized individuals can access sensitive data and services. Multi-factor authentication (MFA) is supported to add an extra layer of security when accessing IBM Cloud accounts. IBM Cloud also provides tools for encryption, allowing organizations to encrypt data at rest and in transit. Data at rest can be protected using IBM Cloud Key Protect, which offers a centralized key management system to securely store and manage encryption keys.

For data in transit, IBM Cloud offers Secure Sockets Layer (SSL)/Transport Layer Security (TLS) support to encrypt data as it travels between users and cloud resources.

To further enhance security, IBM Cloud provides a range of security compliance certifications, such as ISO 27001, SOC 2, and PCI DSS, to demonstrate its commitment to security and compliance. Organizations can leverage these certifications to meet regulatory requirements and build trust with their customers. IBM Cloud also offers threat intelligence and monitoring tools to help organizations detect and respond to security threats in real-time. IBM Cloud Security Advisor provides insights into potential vulnerabilities and offers recommendations for improving security configurations.

Additionally, IBM Cloud Activity Tracker allows organizations to track and audit user activities, providing a detailed log of actions taken within their cloud environment.

Another critical security tool in IBM Cloud is the IBM Cloud Internet Services, which offers Distributed Denial of Service (DDoS) protection and content delivery services to improve the performance and security of web applications.

IBM Cloud Security Groups allow organizations to define network security rules and segment their cloud resources to prevent unauthorized access.

These security groups provide granular control over network traffic, allowing organizations to specify which resources can communicate with each other.

For organizations looking to secure their containerized applications, IBM Cloud Kubernetes Service offers built-in security features such as network policies and pod security policies to control and isolate workloads within a Kubernetes cluster.

IBM Cloud also supports the deployment of virtual private clouds (VPCs) to create isolated network environments, enhancing security and isolation for cloud resources.

To help organizations automate security and compliance, IBM Cloud provides integration with security information and event management (SIEM) solutions like IBM QRadar, enabling organizations to centralize security event monitoring and threat detection.

IBM Cloud Security Advisor also offers integration with IBM Cloud Pak for Security, providing a unified platform for security operations and incident response.

Furthermore, IBM Cloud offers secure and compliant solutions for data storage and database services.

IBM Cloud Hyper Protect DBaaS provides highly secure and scalable database services with built-in encryption and key management, ideal for sensitive data workloads.

IBM Cloud Object Storage enables organizations to store and manage unstructured data securely, with support for data retention and compliance.

Organizations can also leverage IBM Cloud Resilient for incident response and orchestration to streamline and automate their response to security incidents.

For secure application development, IBM Cloud offers tools and services such as IBM Cloud App ID for identity and access management in applications, and IBM Cloud Security Insights to analyze application vulnerabilities.

IBM Cloud DevSecOps tools and practices enable organizations to integrate security into their development and deployment pipelines, ensuring that security is an integral part of the application lifecycle.

To address container security, IBM Cloud Container Registry provides a secure image repository for container images, and IBM Cloud Kubernetes Service offers container security scanning and vulnerability management.

In summary, IBM Cloud offers a comprehensive set of security features and tools to help organizations protect their cloud resources and data.

From identity and access management to encryption, threat detection, compliance certifications, and secure development practices, IBM Cloud provides the tools and capabilities needed to build a secure and compliant cloud environment.

These security features enable organizations to confidently embrace the cloud while safeguarding their data and applications from evolving threats.

Meeting regulatory compliance standards in IBM Cloud is a critical consideration for organizations operating in highly regulated industries such as healthcare, finance, or government.

Regulatory compliance ensures that organizations adhere to specific laws, regulations, and standards governing data security, privacy, and other aspects of their operations.

Failing to meet these compliance requirements can result in legal consequences, fines, and reputational damage.

IBM Cloud offers a range of services and tools to help organizations navigate the complex landscape of regulatory compliance.

One of the fundamental aspects of compliance in IBM Cloud is data protection and privacy.

For organizations handling sensitive personal data, complying with regulations like the General Data Protection Regulation (GDPR) or the Health Insurance Portability and Accountability Act (HIPAA) is essential.

IBM Cloud provides features and services to help organizations meet these requirements, including data encryption, access controls, and auditing capabilities.

Encryption at rest and in transit ensures that sensitive data is protected from unauthorized access.

Access controls and identity and access management (IAM) tools allow organizations to restrict access to data based on user roles and permissions.

Auditing capabilities enable organizations to track and monitor data access and changes, providing an audit trail for compliance purposes.

Additionally, IBM Cloud offers compliance certifications and attestations to demonstrate adherence to industry-specific regulations and standards.

IBM Cloud is certified for compliance with various standards, including ISO 27001, SOC 2, HIPAA, and PCI DSS.

These certifications provide assurance to organizations that IBM Cloud has implemented security controls and practices to protect data and infrastructure.

IBM Cloud also offers compliance documentation and reports that can be shared with auditors and regulators to demonstrate compliance efforts.

For organizations in highly regulated industries, IBM Cloud offers specialized solutions and services designed to meet industry-specific compliance requirements.

For example, IBM Cloud for Financial Services is tailored to address the unique regulatory challenges faced by financial institutions.

This solution includes built-in security and compliance controls aligned with industry standards and regulations.

IBM Cloud for Healthcare offers similar capabilities for organizations in the healthcare sector, helping them achieve compliance with regulations like HIPAA.

Another critical aspect of regulatory compliance is data residency and sovereignty.

Some regulations require that data be stored and processed within specific geographic regions or jurisdictions.

IBM Cloud provides data center locations worldwide, allowing organizations to choose the region that best aligns with their compliance requirements.

IBM Cloud also offers services like IBM Cloud Satellite, which enables organizations to deploy and manage cloud resources in their own data centers or at the edge, providing greater control over data locality.

To assist organizations in their compliance efforts, IBM Cloud offers guidance and best practices for building compliant solutions.

This includes documentation, whitepapers, and reference architectures that outline how to design and configure IBM Cloud services to meet specific compliance requirements.

Organizations can also leverage IBM Cloud Professional Services to assess their compliance posture, identify gaps, and develop a roadmap for achieving and maintaining compliance. In addition to technical controls, compliance often requires organizations to implement policies and procedures that govern how data is handled and protected.

IBM Cloud provides tools for policy management and automation, helping organizations enforce compliance policies consistently across their cloud environment.

IBM Cloud Security Advisor offers insights and recommendations for improving security and compliance configurations.

IBM Cloud Pak for Security provides a unified platform for security operations and incident response, helping organizations detect and respond to compliance-related security incidents.

Furthermore, IBM Cloud supports the principles of shared responsibility in compliance.

While IBM Cloud takes responsibility for the security and compliance of the cloud infrastructure, organizations are responsible for securing their applications and data running on the cloud.

This shared responsibility model means that organizations must implement appropriate security measures within their cloud workloads to maintain compliance.

Ultimately, achieving and maintaining regulatory compliance in IBM Cloud requires a comprehensive approach that encompasses technical controls, documentation, and governance practices.

By leveraging the tools, services, and expertise provided by IBM Cloud, organizations can build and operate compliant solutions that meet their specific regulatory obligations.

This approach not only helps organizations avoid legal and financial penalties but also enhances trust and credibility with customers and partners.

Chapter 7: Advanced Automation with IBM Cloud Services

Leveraging IBM Cloud Automation Manager is a strategic choice for organizations looking to streamline and optimize their cloud management and deployment processes.

IBM Cloud Automation Manager, often referred to as CAM, is a powerful orchestration and automation platform that enables organizations to accelerate their journey towards a more agile and efficient cloud infrastructure.

At its core, CAM provides a range of capabilities that allow organizations to model, deploy, and manage complex cloud environments with ease.

One of the primary benefits of CAM is its ability to abstract the underlying complexity of cloud resources and services, making it easier for IT teams to create and manage cloud resources without delving into the intricacies of cloud provider-specific APIs and configurations.

CAM offers a visual canvas where users can design and customize cloud resources using pre-built templates and blueprints, reducing the time and effort required to deploy and manage cloud infrastructure.

These blueprints encapsulate best practices and design patterns for cloud resources, ensuring that deployments are consistent, compliant, and optimized for performance and cost.

In addition to simplifying cloud resource provisioning, CAM also provides extensive automation capabilities.

Users can define workflows and automation scripts to handle various operational tasks, such as scaling applications based on demand, automating backups, and implementing disaster recovery procedures.

By automating these routine tasks, organizations can improve operational efficiency and reduce the risk of human errors.

Another key feature of CAM is its integration with multiple cloud providers, including IBM Cloud, AWS, Microsoft Azure, and Google Cloud Platform.

This multi-cloud support allows organizations to leverage CAM's capabilities across their hybrid or multi-cloud environments, making it a valuable tool for managing diverse cloud ecosystems.

CAM also provides integration with popular DevOps tools and practices, facilitating the integration of automation and orchestration into existing development and deployment pipelines.

For example, organizations can use CAM to automate the provisioning of development and test environments on-demand, reducing wait times and accelerating the software development lifecycle.

CAM's self-service portal allows end-users and developers to request and manage cloud resources independently, reducing the burden on IT teams and improving agility.

Users can request predefined services and resources from a catalog, and CAM will automate the provisioning and management of these resources, ensuring consistency and compliance.

One of the strengths of CAM is its support for governance and compliance.

Organizations can define policies and controls within CAM to enforce compliance requirements, cost management rules, and security standards.

This ensures that cloud deployments adhere to internal and external regulations, reducing compliance risks.

Additionally, CAM provides monitoring and reporting capabilities to track resource utilization and costs, allowing organizations to optimize their cloud spend and identify opportunities for cost savings.

CAM's extensibility is another notable feature.

Organizations can extend CAM's functionality by creating custom plugins and integrations to meet their specific requirements.

This flexibility makes CAM adaptable to a wide range of use cases, from infrastructure as code (IaC) to application deployment and lifecycle management.

IBM Cloud Automation Manager also supports the concept of "Day 2" operations, which involves ongoing management and optimization of cloud resources.

Organizations can use CAM to automate tasks such as resource scaling, patching, and backup management, ensuring that their cloud environments remain responsive and secure.

Furthermore, CAM's integration with AI and machine learning services allows organizations to leverage predictive analytics to anticipate resource demand and optimize cloud resource allocation.

As organizations continue to embrace cloud computing, the need for efficient cloud management and automation becomes increasingly critical.

IBM Cloud Automation Manager offers a comprehensive solution that empowers organizations to automate and orchestrate cloud resources, streamline operations, and enhance agility.

By abstracting the complexities of cloud provisioning and offering a self-service portal, CAM enables organizations to empower their development teams and accelerate time-to-market.

The ability to integrate with multiple cloud providers and DevOps tools positions CAM as a valuable tool for managing hybrid and multi-cloud environments.

Additionally, CAM's support for governance, compliance, and cost management ensures that organizations can maintain control and transparency over their cloud deployments.

Overall, leveraging IBM Cloud Automation Manager is a strategic move for organizations seeking to harness the full potential of the cloud while maintaining operational excellence and governance.

Infrastructure as Code (IaC) has emerged as a fundamental practice in modern cloud computing, allowing organizations to define and manage their infrastructure using code.

One of the most popular IaC tools in the industry is Terraform, an open-source platform developed by HashiCorp.

Terraform enables users to define and provision infrastructure resources across multiple cloud providers and on-premises environments using a declarative configuration language.

When it comes to managing infrastructure on IBM Cloud, Terraform plays a pivotal role in automating the deployment and configuration of cloud resources.

Terraform's strength lies in its ability to codify infrastructure requirements, making it easy to version, collaborate on, and automate the provisioning of complex cloud environments.

One of the key advantages of using Terraform with IBM Cloud is its support for a wide range of IBM Cloud services and resources.

Terraform providers are available for IBM Cloud, which means users can define and manage IBM Cloud resources directly within Terraform configurations.

This integration simplifies the process of creating and updating IBM Cloud resources while maintaining infrastructure as code.

To get started with Terraform on IBM Cloud, you'll need to install Terraform on your local machine or in your CI/CD pipeline.

Terraform provides official binaries for various operating systems, making it easy to set up.

Once Terraform is installed, you'll need to configure the IBM Cloud provider by specifying your IBM Cloud API key, region, and other relevant information.

This configuration allows Terraform to authenticate and interact with your IBM Cloud account programmatically.

With Terraform properly configured, you can begin defining your infrastructure using HashiCorp Configuration Language (HCL).

HCL is a human-readable and machine-friendly language that makes it easy to express your infrastructure requirements.

Terraform configurations consist of resource blocks that define the desired state of cloud resources.

For example, you can use a resource block to declare the creation of an IBM Cloud Virtual Machine, specifying its size, image, and other attributes.

Terraform also supports module-based development, allowing you to create reusable templates for common infrastructure patterns.

Modules encapsulate Terraform configurations, making it easy to share, version, and reuse infrastructure components across different projects.

Once you've defined your Terraform configurations, you can use Terraform commands to plan and apply changes to your IBM Cloud environment.

The "terraform plan" command examines your configurations and generates an execution plan that outlines the changes Terraform will make to bring your infrastructure to the desired state.

This plan allows you to review the proposed changes and ensure they align with your expectations before applying them.

The "terraform apply" command executes the changes, creating, updating, or deleting resources as necessary to achieve the desired state.

Terraform tracks the state of your infrastructure in a state file, which is used to manage resources and track changes over time.

The state file is a critical component of Terraform's workflow, ensuring that it knows the current state of your infrastructure and can plan changes accordingly.

To collaborate with others on Terraform configurations and manage them more effectively, you can use version control systems like Git.

Storing your Terraform configurations in a Git repository allows you to track changes, collaborate with team members, and maintain a history of your infrastructure changes.

Terraform's ability to define infrastructure as code brings several benefits to managing IBM Cloud resources.

Firstly, it enhances reproducibility, ensuring that you can create identical infrastructure environments across different stages of development and deployment.

This consistency reduces the likelihood of issues arising from configuration discrepancies between environments.

Secondly, Terraform promotes collaboration among development, operations, and infrastructure teams.

By codifying infrastructure requirements, teams can work together more effectively, and infrastructure changes become part of the application's version control and release process.

Thirdly, Terraform provides a robust mechanism for rollback and recovery.

In the event of an issue or error during infrastructure changes, Terraform can revert to the previous known state, reducing downtime and minimizing the impact of errors.

Additionally, Terraform's support for "dry runs" with the "terraform plan" command allows you to assess the potential impact of changes before applying them, reducing the risk of unintended consequences.

Furthermore, Terraform's module system encourages the development of reusable infrastructure components, promoting best practices and consistency across projects.

This modularity simplifies the process of building complex environments by composing smaller, well-defined components.

Terraform's rich ecosystem includes numerous community-contributed modules and extensions, providing pre-built solutions for common use cases.

For organizations using IBM Cloud, Terraform's versatility is a valuable asset.

You can use Terraform to automate the provisioning of virtual machines, databases, storage, and various IBM Cloud services.

This flexibility means that you can manage your entire cloud infrastructure using a single IaC tool, streamlining your operations and reducing manual tasks.

Terraform also integrates seamlessly with other DevOps and automation tools, allowing you to incorporate infrastructure changes into your existing CI/CD pipelines.

This integration enables you to automate the testing, validation, and deployment of infrastructure as part of your application delivery process.

In summary, Infrastructure as Code (IaC) with Terraform on IBM Cloud empowers organizations to manage and automate their cloud infrastructure with precision and consistency.

Terraform's declarative approach to infrastructure provisioning simplifies the management of complex environments and promotes collaboration among teams.

By codifying infrastructure requirements, Terraform enhances reproducibility, rollback capabilities, and the overall reliability of cloud environments.

As organizations continue to embrace cloud computing, Terraform remains a crucial tool for efficiently managing and automating infrastructure on IBM Cloud.

Chapter 8: Enterprise Application Deployment and Integration in IBM Cloud

Deploying and scaling applications in IBM Cloud is a critical aspect of leveraging cloud technology to its full potential.

Modern cloud platforms like IBM Cloud offer a range of tools and services that empower organizations to deploy, manage, and scale applications with agility and efficiency.

Next, we will explore the key concepts, best practices, and techniques for deploying and scaling applications on IBM Cloud.

Application deployment refers to the process of making your software or application available for use by deploying it to a server or cloud infrastructure.

IBM Cloud provides various deployment options, including virtual machines, containers, and serverless computing, to cater to diverse application requirements.

Before deploying an application, it's essential to consider factors such as the application's architecture, resource requirements, scalability needs, and deployment model.

IBM Cloud Virtual Machines (VMs) are a common choice for deploying applications that require full control over the underlying infrastructure.

VMs offer flexibility and can run a wide range of operating systems and software stacks.

Organizations can provision VMs in IBM Cloud and then install and configure their applications as needed.

For highly scalable and containerized applications, IBM Cloud Kubernetes Service (IKS) provides a managed Kubernetes platform that simplifies container orchestration and scaling.

Kubernetes allows you to define the desired state of your application using YAML files and automates the deployment, scaling, and management of containerized workloads.

Serverless computing on IBM Cloud, powered by IBM Cloud Functions, is an excellent option for applications with variable workloads.

Serverless computing abstracts server management, allowing you to focus solely on your code.

It automatically scales your application based on demand, ensuring optimal resource utilization and cost efficiency.

To deploy an application on IBM Cloud, you typically start by creating the necessary infrastructure resources, such as VMs, containers, or serverless functions.

You can use Infrastructure as Code (IaC) tools like Terraform to define and provision your infrastructure programmatically, ensuring consistency and reproducibility.

Once the infrastructure is in place, you can deploy your application code and any required dependencies.

For VM-based deployments, you might use configuration management tools like Ansible or Puppet to automate software installation and configuration.

Containerized applications can be built using containerization platforms like Docker and then deployed to Kubernetes clusters on IBM Cloud.

Serverless applications are typically deployed by defining functions and triggers, which automatically execute in response to events.

IBM Cloud provides various tools and services to facilitate application deployment.

For example, IBM Cloud Continuous Delivery allows you to set up automated pipelines for building, testing, and deploying applications.

These pipelines help streamline the application deployment process and ensure that code changes are tested and deployed reliably.

IBM Cloud also offers integration with popular source code repositories like GitHub, enabling seamless code deployment from source control repositories.

In addition to deploying applications, scaling is a crucial aspect of application management on IBM Cloud.

Scaling refers to the ability to adjust the resources allocated to an application to accommodate changes in workload, traffic, or demand.

IBM Cloud provides several scaling options to meet diverse application needs.

Vertical scaling involves increasing or decreasing the capacity of a single resource, such as a VM or container instance.

You can manually adjust the CPU, memory, and storage resources allocated to an application to handle changes in demand.

Horizontal scaling, on the other hand, involves adding or removing instances of an application to distribute the load and improve availability.

This approach is commonly used with containerized applications running on Kubernetes.

Kubernetes automatically scales the number of container instances based on predefined rules and metrics.

Serverless computing platforms like IBM Cloud Functions inherently offer horizontal scaling, as functions are executed in response to events and automatically scale with demand.

Implementing scaling strategies requires careful planning and monitoring.

You must define scaling triggers and policies that specify when and how resources should be adjusted.

For example, you might set up autoscaling rules that trigger the creation of additional container instances when CPU utilization exceeds a certain threshold.

Monitoring tools like IBM Cloud Monitoring and Application Performance Management (APM) help you track application performance and resource utilization.

These tools provide insights into application health, response times, error rates, and resource consumption.

By continuously monitoring your application, you can make informed decisions about when and how to scale to ensure optimal performance and cost efficiency.

When it comes to deploying and scaling applications on IBM Cloud, best practices are essential for success.

Here are some key best practices to consider:

Start with a well-defined architecture: Before deploying, ensure that your application's architecture is designed for scalability, fault tolerance, and high availability.

Use containerization: Consider containerizing your applications using Docker to simplify deployment and scaling on IBM Cloud Kubernetes Service.

Implement Infrastructure as Code (IaC): Use IaC tools like Terraform to define and provision your infrastructure, making it easy to reproduce and manage.

Automate deployment pipelines: Set up automated deployment pipelines with IBM Cloud Continuous Delivery to streamline the application deployment process.

Leverage scaling triggers: Define scaling triggers and policies based on metrics like CPU utilization, request rate, or custom application metrics to automatically adjust resources.

Monitor and optimize: Continuously monitor your application's performance and resource utilization, and make adjustments based on insights from monitoring tools.

Test for scalability: Perform load testing and scalability testing to ensure your application can handle expected levels of traffic.

Secure your application: Implement security best practices to protect your application and data, and regularly update security configurations.

Backup and disaster recovery: Implement backup and disaster recovery strategies to ensure data availability and application resilience.

Stay cost-conscious: Optimize resource allocation and scaling to minimize costs while maintaining performance.

In summary, deploying and scaling applications on IBM Cloud involves careful planning, infrastructure provisioning, and monitoring.

IBM Cloud offers a range of deployment options and tools to simplify the process, including virtual machines, containers, and serverless computing.

Effective scaling strategies, coupled with best practices in architecture, automation, and security, are crucial for ensuring that applications run smoothly and efficiently in the cloud.

Integration solutions play a pivotal role in connecting and coordinating various services and applications within the IBM Cloud ecosystem.

These solutions enable organizations to streamline their business processes, enhance data sharing, and improve overall efficiency.

Next, we will delve into the integration solutions available for IBM Cloud services and how they facilitate seamless communication and data exchange.

IBM Cloud offers a comprehensive set of integration solutions to meet the diverse needs of modern enterprises.

One of the core integration services provided by IBM Cloud is IBM App Connect, a versatile platform that connects applications, data, and APIs across cloud and on-premises environments.

IBM App Connect allows organizations to design, develop, and deploy integration flows that automate workflows, synchronize data, and trigger actions in response to events.

With a user-friendly interface and a wide range of connectors, IBM App Connect empowers both technical and non-technical users to create integrations quickly.

For organizations looking to connect and orchestrate cloud-based services, IBM Cloud Integration provides a robust and scalable solution.

This platform supports hybrid integrations, making it possible to connect cloud services with on-premises systems and applications.

IBM Cloud Integration leverages industry-standard technologies like Apache Camel and Apache Kafka to facilitate the seamless flow of data and events.

It also offers a visual integration development environment for building integration flows.

For enterprises seeking an event-driven architecture, IBM Event Streams provides a managed Kafka service that simplifies the deployment and management of event-driven applications.

Kafka is a powerful platform for building real-time data pipelines and streaming applications.

IBM Event Streams offers features like automatic scaling, encryption, and multi-region availability, making it an ideal choice for building event-driven systems on IBM Cloud.

In addition to these services, IBM Cloud provides API management solutions that enable organizations to create, publish, and manage APIs.

IBM API Connect allows businesses to expose their data and services securely while enforcing policies for authentication, rate limiting, and access control.

This solution simplifies API development, documentation, and testing, accelerating the API lifecycle.

For organizations adopting a microservices architecture, IBM Cloud Kubernetes Service (IKS) plays a vital role in facilitating the deployment and management of microservices.

IKS provides a managed Kubernetes platform that automates container orchestration, scaling, and updates.

Kubernetes, coupled with containerization technologies like Docker, empowers organizations to build, deploy, and scale microservices efficiently.

IBM Cloud Kubernetes Service also offers integration with Istio, an open-source service mesh that enhances security, observability, and traffic management for microservices.

As enterprises embrace cloud-native development practices, serverless computing becomes increasingly popular.

IBM Cloud Functions is an event-driven serverless computing platform that allows organizations to execute code in response to events.

Developers can create serverless functions that respond to various events, such as HTTP requests, database changes, or IoT sensor data.

IBM Cloud Functions automatically scales the execution environment, ensuring optimal resource utilization and cost efficiency.

When it comes to data integration and analytics, IBM Cloud offers IBM Cloud Pak for Data, an integrated data and AI platform.

This platform allows organizations to collect, organize, and analyze data from various sources while providing AI-powered insights.

IBM Cloud Pak for Data includes data integration capabilities, data governance, and AI-powered data cataloging, making it a comprehensive solution for data-driven organizations.

For businesses that rely on enterprise resource planning (ERP) systems, IBM Cloud Integration for SAP provides pre-built connectors and templates to streamline SAP integrations with other applications and services.

This integration solution simplifies the orchestration of business processes involving SAP systems.

Furthermore, IBM Cloud supports the integration of blockchain technology into business processes.

IBM Blockchain Platform allows organizations to create, deploy, and manage blockchain networks.

Blockchain technology enables secure and transparent data sharing across distributed networks, making it suitable for use cases such as supply chain management, provenance tracking, and digital identity.

In summary, IBM Cloud offers a rich array of integration solutions to connect and coordinate services and applications within the cloud ecosystem.

From integration platforms like IBM App Connect and IBM Cloud Integration to event-driven solutions like IBM Event Streams and serverless computing with IBM Cloud Functions, organizations can choose the integration approach that best fits their needs.

Additionally, IBM Cloud provides API management, microservices orchestration, data integration, and blockchain solutions to support a wide range of use cases and business requirements.

These integration capabilities empower organizations to optimize their business processes, improve data sharing, and drive innovation in a rapidly evolving digital landscape.

Chapter 9: Cost Optimization and Resource Governance

Effective cost management is a critical aspect of any organization's cloud computing strategy, and IBM Cloud offers several strategies to help businesses optimize their cloud expenditures.

Next, we will explore various cost management strategies and best practices for maximizing the value of IBM Cloud services.

IBM Cloud provides a range of tools and features to help organizations monitor and control their cloud spending.

One fundamental aspect of cost management is cost visibility, and IBM Cloud offers a detailed billing and usage dashboard that allows users to track their cloud expenditures.

This dashboard provides insights into resource consumption, costs by service, and usage trends, helping organizations understand where their cloud budget is being allocated.

By gaining visibility into their cloud expenses, organizations can identify areas where optimization is needed.

One common cost management practice is to leverage reserved instances or reserved virtual servers.

IBM Cloud offers Reserved Virtual Server Instances, which allow users to reserve specific virtual server configurations in advance for a fixed period, typically one or three years.

By committing to these reservations, organizations can benefit from significant cost savings compared to on-demand pricing.

Reserved instances are an excellent choice for workloads with predictable usage patterns and long-term commitments.

Another cost-saving option is IBM Cloud Flex Pools, which provide a flexible way to allocate cloud resources across multiple services.

With Flex Pools, organizations can purchase a pool of resources, such as virtual CPUs and memory, and then allocate those resources dynamically to various services within IBM Cloud.

This flexibility allows organizations to optimize resource allocation based on the specific needs of different workloads, resulting in cost savings.

To further optimize costs, organizations can take advantage of IBM Cloud's pay-as-you-go pricing model.

With this model, organizations only pay for the resources they use, with no upfront commitments or long-term contracts. This flexibility is ideal for workloads with varying demand patterns, as it allows organizations to scale resources up or down as needed.

IBM Cloud also offers resource tagging capabilities, which enable organizations to label resources with custom metadata. By tagging resources based on their purpose, project, or department, organizations can gain better insights into how resources are being used and allocate costs more accurately. Resource tagging is particularly valuable for large enterprises with complex cloud environments.

Another cost management strategy is to leverage IBM Cloud's cost and usage reports, which provide granular details on resource consumption and spending.

These reports can be customized to align with an organization's cost allocation and show usage patterns over time.

By analyzing these reports, organizations can identify underutilized resources, optimize resource allocation, and implement cost-saving measures.

IBM Cloud also offers recommendations and cost management insights through the IBM Cloud Cost and Asset Management service.

This service provides tailored recommendations to help organizations reduce costs by identifying areas where optimization is possible.

Additionally, organizations can set up cost budgets and alerts to proactively monitor spending and receive notifications when expenses exceed predefined thresholds.

Furthermore, organizations can take advantage of IBM Cloud's enterprise agreement options, such as the IBM Cloud Agreement for Enterprise or the IBM Cloud Agreement for Partners.

These agreements provide cost-saving incentives and pricing structures tailored to the specific needs of larger organizations or partners.

By negotiating custom agreements with IBM Cloud, organizations can access additional cost benefits.

Incorporating automation into cost management practices is also essential for optimizing cloud expenditures.

IBM Cloud offers automation tools and capabilities, such as IBM Cloud Schematics and Terraform, which allow organizations to automate resource provisioning and scaling.

Automating resource management ensures that resources are only active when needed, reducing unnecessary costs.

Another important aspect of cost management is rightsizing, which involves selecting the appropriate resource configurations to match workload requirements.

IBM Cloud offers resource sizing recommendations to help organizations choose the right mix of CPU, memory, and storage for their workloads.

Rightsizing ensures that resources are neither overprovisioned nor underutilized, leading to cost savings.

To further control costs, organizations can implement cost allocation and chargeback mechanisms using IBM Cloud's cost management features.

These mechanisms enable organizations to allocate cloud expenses to different departments, projects, or teams based on resource usage.

This transparency helps in accountability and encourages responsible cloud spending.

Lastly, organizations can take advantage of cost management consulting services offered by IBM Cloud.

These services provide expert guidance and recommendations for optimizing cloud costs, identifying cost-saving opportunities, and implementing best practices.

IBM Cloud's team of experts can work closely with organizations to develop a tailored cost management strategy.

In summary, effective cost management in IBM Cloud is crucial for organizations seeking to maximize the value of their cloud investments.

By gaining visibility into their cloud expenses, leveraging reserved instances and flexible resource allocation, adopting pay-as-you-go pricing, implementing resource tagging and automation, analyzing cost and usage reports, and incorporating rightsizing and cost allocation practices, organizations can optimize their cloud expenditures and achieve better cost control.

Additionally, IBM Cloud offers consulting services and cost management insights to help organizations continuously improve their cost management strategies and drive value from their cloud investments.

Resource governance is a critical aspect of managing cloud resources effectively and ensuring that they are used in compliance with organizational policies and standards. In IBM Cloud, implementing resource governance policies involves defining rules and constraints that govern how cloud resources are provisioned, used, and managed within an organization's cloud environment. These policies are essential for maintaining control over resource usage, optimizing costs, ensuring security and compliance, and aligning cloud operations with business objectives.

One of the key components of resource governance in IBM Cloud is the use of resource groups. Resource groups provide a logical grouping of cloud resources based on various criteria, such as business units, projects, or applications. By organizing resources into resource groups, organizations can enforce governance policies at a granular level and manage resources more efficiently.

Resource groups in IBM Cloud also allow organizations to define access controls and permissions. Access policies can be established to determine who can create, modify, or delete resources within a resource group. This fine-grained control ensures that only authorized personnel can make changes to cloud resources, reducing the risk of unauthorized actions that could lead to security breaches or compliance violations.

Resource tagging is another essential aspect of resource governance in IBM Cloud. Tags are user-defined metadata that can be associated with cloud resources to provide additional context and categorization. Organizations can create tag categories and assign tags to resources based on criteria such as cost centers, owners, environments, or compliance requirements. Tagging enables organizations to track resource usage, allocate costs accurately, and enforce governance policies based on tags.

IBM Cloud offers a Policy Management service that allows organizations to define and enforce governance policies across their cloud environment. Policies can be created to control various aspects of resource provisioning and management, such as resource type, location, size, and naming conventions. For example, organizations can create policies that require all virtual machines to be tagged with specific cost center tags or enforce naming conventions for cloud resources.

The Policy Management service in IBM Cloud also supports custom policy templates, enabling organizations to define their own policy rules based on their specific requirements. These templates can be shared across resource groups and projects, ensuring consistent policy enforcement throughout the organization.

Resource quotas and limits are another governance mechanism provided by IBM Cloud. Quotas specify the maximum number of resources that can be provisioned within a resource group or project, while limits define thresholds for resource usage. By setting quotas and limits, organizations can prevent resource overprovisioning, control costs, and ensure that cloud resources are used efficiently.

IBM Cloud Identity and Access Management (IAM) plays a crucial role in resource governance by managing user access and permissions. IAM policies can be defined to grant or restrict access to specific cloud resources based on user roles and responsibilities. This ensures that only authorized individuals or teams can perform actions on resources and helps organizations maintain control over their cloud environment.

Resource monitoring and auditing are integral to resource governance in IBM Cloud. Organizations can use the IBM Cloud Activity Tracker to monitor resource-related events and activities. This tool provides detailed audit logs that capture changes made to resources, access events, and policy violations. These logs can be used for compliance reporting, security investigations, and identifying potential governance issues.

IBM Cloud also offers integration with external compliance and governance tools, allowing organizations to extend their resource governance practices beyond the cloud platform. By integrating with these tools, organizations can perform continuous compliance assessments, enforce security policies, and maintain alignment with industry-specific regulations and standards.

Another important aspect of resource governance in IBM Cloud is cost management. Organizations can use cost management tools and reports to gain insights into resource spending, allocate costs to resource groups or projects, and track budget adherence. Cost management is a critical component of governance, as it ensures that cloud resources are used efficiently and cost-effectively.

To implement resource governance policies effectively, organizations should establish a governance team responsible for defining, enforcing, and monitoring policies. This team should work closely with cloud administrators, developers, and other stakeholders to ensure that policies are aligned with business goals and that governance practices are consistently applied.

In summary, implementing resource governance policies in IBM Cloud is essential for organizations to maintain control over their cloud resources, optimize costs, ensure security and compliance, and align cloud operations with business objectives. By leveraging resource groups, access controls, tagging, policy management, quotas, limits, IAM, monitoring, auditing, cost management, and external integrations, organizations can establish robust governance practices that support their cloud journey. Resource governance is an ongoing process that requires collaboration across teams and continuous monitoring and adjustment to align with evolving business needs and regulatory requirements.

Chapter 10: Real-World Enterprise Success Stories with IBM Cloud

In today's rapidly evolving business landscape, enterprises are constantly seeking ways to stay competitive, agile, and innovative. One significant aspect of achieving these goals is the transformation of their IT infrastructure. This case study delves into the journey of a large enterprise that successfully transformed its IT operations by embracing IBM Cloud.

The Challenge:

The enterprise in question, a global organization with a diverse portfolio of products and services, faced several challenges in its existing IT environment. It operated a complex on-premises infrastructure that was becoming increasingly difficult to manage and scale. The IT team struggled to keep up with the demands of the business, leading to delays in provisioning resources, high operational costs, and limited flexibility to adapt to market changes.

The Transformation Journey:

Recognizing the need for change, the enterprise embarked on a comprehensive IT transformation journey with IBM Cloud as a key enabler. The transformation goals included:

Scalability: The enterprise aimed to build an IT infrastructure that could scale seamlessly to support its growing business operations. IBM Cloud's elastic and scalable resources provided the foundation for achieving this goal.

Cost Optimization: Controlling IT costs was a top priority. By moving to a pay-as-you-go model with IBM Cloud, the enterprise could optimize its spending and reduce capital expenditures.

Speed and Agility: The ability to rapidly provision and deploy resources was critical. IBM Cloud's self-service capabilities allowed teams to provision virtual machines, databases, and other resources in minutes rather than weeks.

Security and Compliance: As a global enterprise, maintaining robust security and compliance standards was non-negotiable. IBM Cloud's comprehensive security features and compliance certifications ensured that data and applications remained protected.

Business Continuity: The enterprise needed a disaster recovery and business continuity plan. IBM Cloud's geographically dispersed data centers and built-in redundancy provided the required resilience.

Innovation: Staying ahead in the market required fostering innovation. IBM Cloud's support for emerging technologies, such as AI, machine learning, and IoT, allowed the enterprise to explore new opportunities.

The Implementation:

The enterprise's transformation journey began with a thorough assessment of its existing IT environment. It identified workloads suitable for migration to the cloud, prioritizing those with the greatest impact on business operations. IBM Cloud's Migration Services played a pivotal role in executing the migration seamlessly.

During the migration, the enterprise leveraged IBM Cloud's hybrid cloud capabilities. This approach allowed it to retain some critical workloads on-premises while gradually transitioning others to the cloud. The hybrid architecture ensured a smooth transition without disrupting ongoing operations.

IBM Cloud's extensive catalog of services further accelerated the transformation. The enterprise adopted cloud-native development practices and microservices architecture to modernize its applications. IBM Cloud Kubernetes Service provided a container orchestration platform for deploying and managing these modernized applications.

To enhance collaboration and communication, the enterprise adopted IBM Cloud services for messaging, collaboration, and video conferencing. These tools facilitated remote work and improved productivity across the organization.

The Results:

The enterprise's transformation with IBM Cloud yielded remarkable results:

Cost Savings: By migrating to IBM Cloud's pay-as-you-go model, the enterprise reduced capital expenditures and achieved significant cost savings.

Agility: Teams could provision resources and deploy applications much faster, enabling them to respond quickly to business demands and market changes.

Scalability: IBM Cloud's elastic infrastructure allowed the enterprise to scale resources up or down as needed, ensuring optimal performance and resource utilization.

Security: IBM Cloud's robust security features and compliance certifications bolstered the enterprise's security posture, instilling confidence among customers and partners.

Business Continuity: The enterprise's disaster recovery plan, powered by IBM Cloud, ensured business continuity even in the face of unforeseen disruptions.

Innovation: With access to IBM Cloud's cutting-edge technologies, the enterprise explored new avenues for innovation, enhancing its competitive edge.

Improved Collaboration: IBM Cloud's collaboration tools promoted seamless communication and collaboration among employees, regardless of their locations.

In summary, the enterprise's transformation journey with IBM Cloud exemplifies the potential for organizations to overcome complex IT challenges and drive innovation while maintaining security and compliance. By embracing the scalability, cost-effectiveness, and agility of IBM Cloud, enterprises can position themselves for sustained success in a rapidly evolving digital landscape.

In today's highly competitive business landscape, achieving sustained growth is a top priority for enterprises of all sizes. This case study delves into the journey of a medium-sized company that successfully leveraged IBM Cloud solutions to drive business growth and enhance its overall competitiveness.

The Business Landscape:

The company in question, which operates in the retail industry, had experienced steady growth over the years. However, it faced several challenges that were inhibiting its ability to expand further. These challenges included:

Limited Scalability: The company's existing IT infrastructure was struggling to support the increasing demands of its expanding operations.

Inefficient Operations: Manual processes and outdated legacy systems were causing operational inefficiencies and delays.

Customer Experience: The company recognized the importance of providing a seamless and personalized customer experience but struggled to do so with its existing technology stack.

Competitive Pressure: The retail industry was becoming increasingly competitive, with new entrants and established players offering innovative services and experiences.

The Transformation Objectives:

To address these challenges and achieve sustainable growth, the company defined several key objectives for its transformation journey:

Scalability: The company needed an IT infrastructure that could easily scale to accommodate its growth without incurring excessive costs.

Operational Efficiency: Automation and streamlined processes were crucial to improving operational efficiency and reducing manual errors.

Enhanced Customer Experience: The company aimed to deliver a more personalized and engaging customer experience, both online and in-store.

Competitive Edge: To stay ahead of competitors, the company sought to leverage technology to offer unique services and promotions to its customers.

Data-Driven Decision-Making: The company recognized the value of data and analytics in making informed business decisions.

The Implementation:

The company decided to partner with IBM to embark on its digital transformation journey. IBM offered a comprehensive suite of cloud solutions that aligned with the company's objectives:

Scalability with IBM Cloud: The company migrated its existing IT infrastructure to IBM Cloud, taking advantage of the platform's elasticity to scale resources up or down based on demand.

Operational Efficiency with Automation: IBM's automation capabilities allowed the company to streamline its processes, reducing manual work and errors.

Enhanced Customer Experience with AI: IBM Watson, the AI-powered platform, was used to develop chatbots and virtual shopping assistants that provided personalized recommendations to customers.

Competitive Edge with Mobile Apps: IBM MobileFirst Platform enabled the development of mobile apps that allowed customers to browse products, receive special offers, and make purchases conveniently.

Data Analytics with IBM Cloud Pak for Data: The company leveraged data analytics to gain insights into customer behavior, inventory management, and market trends, enabling data-driven decision-making.

The Results:

The company's strategic transformation with IBM Cloud solutions yielded significant results:

Scalability: The company was now able to seamlessly scale its infrastructure to accommodate increased traffic and demand during peak seasons.

Operational Efficiency: Automation reduced operational costs and errors, allowing employees to focus on more strategic tasks.

Enhanced Customer Experience: Personalized recommendations and virtual shopping assistants improved the customer journey, resulting in higher customer satisfaction and retention.

Competitive Edge: The mobile app and innovative services attracted new customers and kept existing ones engaged, giving the company a competitive edge.

Data-Driven Insights: With data analytics, the company could make informed decisions regarding inventory, marketing campaigns, and product offerings, optimizing its operations.

Business Growth: The company experienced significant revenue growth as a result of these improvements, solidifying its position in the market.

In summary, this case study illustrates how a medium-sized retail company harnessed the power of IBM Cloud solutions to overcome challenges, achieve its transformation objectives, and drive business growth. By embracing scalability, automation, AI, and data analytics, the company not only improved its operations but also enhanced the overall customer experience, ultimately leading to increased competitiveness and success in the dynamic retail industry.

Conclusion

In this comprehensive book bundle, "IaaS Mastery: Infrastructure as a Service," we embarked on a journey through the intricate world of cloud infrastructure. Across four distinct volumes, we covered everything from the fundamental concepts to advanced architectures, providing you with a holistic understanding of Infrastructure as a Service (IaaS). Let's take a moment to reflect on the key takeaways from this bundle.

Book 1 - IaaS Fundamentals: A Beginner's Guide to Cloud Infrastructure:

In this foundational volume, we laid the groundwork for your IaaS journey. We introduced you to the fundamental principles of cloud computing, demystifying complex concepts and terminology. You gained a clear understanding of the benefits of IaaS and its role in modern IT landscapes. By the end of this book, you were well-prepared to embark on your cloud infrastructure journey.

Book 2 - Mastering IaaS: Building Scalable Cloud Solutions with AWS and GCE:

Building upon the fundamentals, the second book in the series delved into the practical aspects of IaaS using two major cloud providers: Amazon Web Services (AWS) and Google Cloud Engine (GCE). You learned how to create scalable and resilient cloud solutions, harnessing the power of these platforms. The emphasis was on hands-on experience, ensuring you could confidently deploy and manage resources in the cloud.

Book 3 - Advanced IaaS Architectures: Optimizing Microsoft Azure for Enterprises:

In the third volume, we explored the vast capabilities of Microsoft Azure, specifically tailored for enterprise solutions. You delved into advanced IaaS architectures, focusing on optimizing Azure for enterprise-grade workloads. Topics like high-performance networks, scalable compute solutions, advanced security, and automation were at the forefront. By the end of this book, you were well-equipped to tackle complex enterprise challenges in the Azure ecosystem.

Book 4 - IaaS Expertise: Harnessing the Power of IBM Cloud for Enterprise Solutions:

The final book in the bundle elevated your expertise to the next level by uncovering the potential of IBM Cloud for enterprise solutions. You explored IBM's infrastructure offerings, networking strategies, security features, and advanced automation capabilities. With a deep dive into real-world enterprise success stories, you gained insights into how IBM Cloud could drive transformation within large organizations.

As we conclude this book bundle, you now possess a comprehensive knowledge of IaaS and the capabilities of major cloud providers, including AWS, GCE, Microsoft Azure, and IBM Cloud. Whether you are a beginner looking to understand the basics or an experienced professional seeking to optimize cloud infrastructure for enterprises, this bundle has provided you with the essential insights and practical skills to succeed in the dynamic world of cloud computing.

With the ever-evolving landscape of cloud technology, your journey in mastering IaaS is ongoing. We encourage you to stay curious, explore new innovations, and continue refining your expertise. The possibilities in the cloud are boundless, and your mastery of IaaS opens doors to endless opportunities for innovation, efficiency, and growth in the digital age.

www.ingramcontent.com/pod-product-compliance
Lightning Source LLC
Chambersburg PA
CBHW071235050326
40690CB00011B/2122